The Right Angle Club

Annual Report 2017

Copyright © 2017

Printed by Ross & Perry, Inc., 2017

© Ross & Perry, Inc., 2017 on new material. All rights reserved.

Printed in the United States of America

Ross & Perry, Inc. Publishers
3 South Haddon Avenue, Suite 4
Haddonfield, N.J. 08033
Telephone (856) 427-6135
Facsimile (856) 427-6136
Visit us at www.rossperry.com
http://www.rossperry.com

ISBN 10: 1-932109-53-6
ISBN 13: 978-1-932109-53-5

Book cover and interior design by Creative Publishing Book Design

All rights reserved. No copyrighted part of this publication may be reproduced or transmitted in any form or by any means, electronic or mechanical, including photocopying, recording, or by any information storage and retrieval system without prior written permission of the publisher.

*Dick Palmer and Bill Dorsey died this year.
We will miss them.*

Table of Contents

TOPIC 384 Right Angle Club 2017

BLOG 3826	The Right Angle President Letter: Wayne R. Strasbaugh	1
BLOG 760	Look Out For That Ship!	2
BLOG 3825	Bill Dorsey: Death of a former President	4
BLOG 941	Pirate Lair	5
BLOG 3712	The Zimmerman Telegram	6
BLOG 3701	Uncorking the Past	7
BLOG 3730	The Wistars Think Big, But Talk Softly	8
BLOG 3698	The Burdens of the Rich	10
BLOG 3711	Ethnic Cemeteries	11
BLOG 3713	Deputy Managing Director	13
BLOG 3714	Suited To A "T"	14
BLOG 3717	Post-Graduate Medical Education in Philadelphia	15
BLOG 3727	(1) Medicine at the Two Ends of Life: First year of Life, and Last Years of Life.	17
BLOG 3728	(2) Death as a Portion of Lifetime Health Expense	19
BLOG 3722	Two Central Mistakes In The Design of Health Insurance	20
BLOG 3600	Paying for Medicare Transition with Trust Funds	22
BLOG 3759	Broad Brush	24
BLOG 3695	Currencies Owned by Nations, or by People?	25
BLOG 3716	Uber and 215 Get A Cab	27
BLOG 1008	The Definition of a Real Philadelphian (1914)	28
BLOG 3718	Two Central Mistakes In The Design of Medicare.	29
BLOG 3731	De-Globalization: Is It Real? Compared With War, Is It Cheap?	31
BLOG 3737	Award Seminar # 3940: Douglas C. Wallace, PhD	32
BLOG 3725	College for Prison Inmates	34
BLOG 3726	Awbury	36
BLOG 3715	Dracula	37

BLOG 3693	Passive Investing With Total-Market Index Funds	38
BLOG 3685	The Future of Index-fund Investing, Itself	39
BLOG 3694	Equities, Not Debt	41
BLOG 3729	Girard College as an Entertainment Site	43
BLOG 2930	New Looks for College?	45
BLOG 3471	"Sir"	46
BLOG 3225	Pickett›s Charge	48
BLOG 3736	Franklin Institute Awards Week	50
BLOG 3735	Aaron Burr: Good Guy, or Skunk?	52
BLOG 2379	Conowingo	55
BLOG 980	Emperor›s Doctor	57
BLOG 970	Rufus Jones, Quaker	57
BLOG 3724	Bedroom City?	58
BLOG 1219	Native Habitat	59
BLOG 3791	What›s Wrong With our Airport?	62
BLOG 3746	Let›s Annex Canada	63
BLOG 1493	Buying Corporate America with Cheap Money	64
BLOG 3747	Is There Any Other Medical Revenue?	65
BLOG 3668	The Plan	66
BLOG 1639	Steep Yield-Curves Subsidize Banks	69
BLOG 3734	The Marriage of Figaro, Huzzah!	71
BLOG 3723	Hepatitis C Has Been Cured: Tell All Your Friends	72
BLOG 3480	Reflections on Immortality	74
BLOG 3508	The Stamp Tax: Highly Innovative, Much Underestimated	74
BLOG 3524	After London, Ben Franklin Revisited	76
BLOG 3544	Innovation and Automation	78
BLOG 3578	Franklin and Brexit	79
BLOG 2663	Honoring the Fallen	80
BLOG 3757	Michael Dell, the Millionaire Teen-ager	82
BLOG 3761	Azaleas and Rhodedendrons at Tyler Arboretum	83
BLOG 3819	Artificial Intelligence	84
BLOG 3804	Quakers and Idolatry	85
BLOG 3760	Fraud and Abuse in Medicare and Other Government Programs	86

BLOG 3758	The Lawsuit That Ate Philadelphia	87
BLOG 3486	Suggested Additions	89
BLOG 3497	H.I.V., AIDS, and the Law	90
BLOG 3487	Exit Strategy: Medicare as the First Pearl in the HSA Necklace	92
BLOG 3506	Getting Started	94
BLOG 3513	Looking a Gift Horse in the Mouth	95
BLOG 3669	How to Live a Long Life and Get Rich	98
BLOG 3741	Rescuing Medicare from Its Short-Term Thinking	99
BLOG 3818	Tax Legislation--Just A Condominium Squabble	101
BLOG 3502	Revolutionary Features of Big Data	102

The Right Angle President Letter: Wayne R. Strasbaugh

Fellow Right Anglers, As we conclude 2017, it is with pleasure that I submit this report. Our 95th year was marked with the good camaraderie and fellowship that has forever characterized our Club. Unfortunately, it was also a year in which we have had to bid farewell to our former presidents Otis Erisman and Bill Dorsey and longtime members Bob Gill, Dick Palmer and Alan Lawley. As we begin the New Year, let us remember these gentlemen and their contributions to the Right Angle.

The year began with our adopting amendments to our Constitution and Bylaws designed to conform them to our current practices and procedures. The new position of Membership Secretary was created to provide more focus to our recruitment efforts. The position of Corresponding Secretary, a relic of the pre-internet age, was abolished.

As we enjoyed good food and views of the Philadelphia skyline for the second year at our new Pyramid Club venue, we listened to speakers present a variety of topics - contemporary and historical, cultural and scientific. We may once again justly boast that no one is better informed about the past, present and future of the Philadelphia area than the members of the Right Angle Club. At two of our lunches, one in March and one in November, we shared these learning opportunities with our lady guests.

Our extracurricular events included the Spring Fling at the Philadelphia Armory, where we were treated to a special tour of the artifacts of the First City Troop, and the Fall Fling at the Headquarters House of the

National Society of The Colonial Dames of America in the Commonwealth of Pennsylvania. Finally, the year was capped with a festive Christmas Party at the Acorn Club.

None of these events could have taken place without the contributions of many Club members. In particular, I would like to acknowledge the loyal support I have received from our First Vice President Chad Bardone, who was always willing to fill my place on short notice. Our Second Vice President John Coates deserves kudos for his choice of venues for the Flings and for the Christmas Party, and our Third Vice President Morris Klein credit for pursuing and scheduling our luncheon speakers. Fourth Vice President Bob Lohr efficiently ran an honest lottery.

Treasurer Tom Williams continued to show his mastery of budgets and figures in keeping the Club on a firm financial footing. Recording Secretary Stephen Clowery and Archivist Steve Bennett compiled and preserved Club records for succeeding generations of Right Anglers. Membership Secretary Dan Sossaman II stalked the city and suburbs for prospects who would learn of our deeds by joining the Club. At large Board of Control Members Scott Inglis, Bob Haskell, Sam Weaver and Jack Foltz testified to the truth of Woody Allen's adage that "80% of success is just showing up."

I would also be remiss if I did not also acknowledge the willingness of Tom Howes to compensate for the Club President's lack of humor by sharing his words of wisdom with us every week.

Finally, I would like to thank George Fisher for the time and effort he expends every year in producing this Annual Report.

Wayne R. Strasbaugh
President 2017

TOPIC 384 Right Angle Club 2017 => BLOG 760 Look Out For That Ship!

Look Out For That Ship!

Tales of the Sea abound, even a hundred miles from the ocean.

We are indebted to the President of the Maritime Law Association of the U.S., Richard W. Palmer, Esq. (who unfortunately died in March 2017 at the age of 97), for both a strange definition, and an amusing story. An "allision" is a collision between a ship and a stationary object, such as a bridge or a dock. As you might imagine, the ship is almost invariably at fault, mainly through errors of the pilot, although hurricanes and other severe weather conditions can make a difference. Moving ships have been running into stationary objects for many centuries, and almost every allision contingency has been explored. Ho hum for maritime law.

The Delair railroad drawbridge over the Delaware River at Frankford Junction is just a little different. It was built in 1896 when the Pennsylvania RR decided it needed to veer off from its North East Corridor to take people to Atlantic City. For reasons relating to the afterthought nature of the bridge, the tower for the drawbridge is located half a mile away, out of direct vision of the ships going through. Also, a late development in the history of the river was the construction of U.S. Steel's Morristown plant, bringing unexpectedly huge ore boats from Labrador to the steel mill. The captains of the ships pretty much turned things over to the river pilots, for the last hundred miles of the trip.

> Tales of the Sea abound, even a hundred miles from the ocean.

Shortly after this iron ore service was begun, the inaugural ore boat Captain had a little party with some invited guests. So it happened that the Commandant of the Port, the Admiral in Charge of the Naval Yard, and other equally high ranking worthies like the head of the Coast Guard were on the bridge of the ore boat, taking careful notes of the procedure.

Delair Railroad Drawbridge

The ship tooted three times, the shore answered back with three toots. In real fact, they were connected by ship-to-shore telephone for most of the real business, but this grand occasion called for authentic nautical ceremony. Three toots, we're approaching your bridge. Three toots back, come ahead, the coast is clear. The admirals scribbled it all down.

As the ship approached the point of no-return, beyond which it could no longer stop or turn in time to avoid an "allision", the people on the bridge were appalled to see a train crossing the bridge ahead. Several toots, loud profanity on the ship to shore phone.

No worry, answered the bridge, we'll lift the drawbridge in plenty of time. But half a minute later the bridge controller made the anguished cry that the drawbridge was apparently rusted and wouldn't open, to which the captain shouted, "This ship is going to take away your blinkety blank bridge and sail right through it".

At this point, the pilot took matters into his own hands, and violently threw the rudder hard left, swinging the ship sideways, soon nudging the bridge with some damage, but nothing like the damage of a head on allision. Lawsuit, as one might imagine, was the outcome.

The attorneys for the railroad were pretty high-powered, too, and had piles of legal precedents to cite. But they were quite unprepared for Dick Palmer to put the Commandant of the Port on the witness stand, reading slowly and painfully from his very detailed notes about the conversations on the bridge, about the approaching drawbridge.

And so, Philadelphia can now claim to have experienced one of the very few instances where a ship ran into a bridge -- and the court found the bridge to be entirely at fault.

Bill Dorsey: Death of a former President

William G. Dorsey

Philadelphia is a city of rivers, so it is not surprising that membership and presidency of the club sometimes has a nautical tint. This year, Bill Dorsey the President of the Delaware River Pilots Association and a former President of the Right Angle Club, died at the Quaker Retirement Community in Kennett Square called Kendall. He was a joyful presence in the club, and will be much missed.

The Right Angle Club is a dressy one, but not many members realize that dressiness is part of the tradition of the Delaware River Pilots Association. When the pilot transfers from the pilot boat in Lewes Delaware to climb the rope ladder into the incoming vessel, it has been traditional for centuries for him to be dressed for a state occasion. Regardless of the weather, it is traditional for the pilot to be piped aboard, dressed in formal clothes. We have a photo of Cap'n Bill, dressed in blue serge pinstripes, climbing up the side of a Labrador iron ore bulk cargo in Lewes, and quite obviously enjoying the experience.

The pilot association is an exclusive organization, often requiring hereditary status, as is often true of trade Unions which date back to medieval times. But they have to know their stuff, always anticipating the possibility of a court appearance with millions of dollars at stake. That is particularly true in port cities with a long estuary, which in Philadelphia's case is over a hundred miles long. Bill, like many officers and port wardens, was active in Delaware politics, and lived in one of a row of pilot mansions along the canal from Lewes to Rehoboth, Delaware. This combination of the raucous conviviality of a trade union politician, together with the utter seriousness of guiding a multi-million dollar ocean ship up a hundred miles of shoals, is approached somewhat by the conflicts of the pilots of ocean-spanning airline pilots with the reckless fearlessness required in their trade.

Delaware River Pilots Association

Bill and I were conceivably related. Or at least in the Eighteenth Century the chartmaker of the mouth of the Delaware was one Joshua Fisher, expelled from his profession when he refused to stop charting the Delaware out of fear that one of those charts would fall into the hands of the British Navy. Joshua then moved to the banks of the Schuylkill and his family disappeared when revolution was declared; no one has seriously investigated this vaporous history. Like so much folklore, more people would probably be happier if much of it were allowed to float away.

TOPIC 384 Right Angle Club 2017 => BLOG 941 Pirate Lair

Pirate Lair

Jolly Roger Flag

Did Blackbeard use the Delaware marshes as a hideout?
The Delaware takes a ninety degree turn right at about the place where the Salem nuclear cooling towers are visible on the Jersey shore, and great quantities of silt have piled up in the river there, making marshes and swamps. There is a rumor that Captain Kidd tied up among these marshy islands, and much better evidence that Blackbeard the Pirate used the Delaware marshes as a hideout. Since a high-speed highway, with limited access, now rushes visitors to the slot machines of Dover and the beaches of Lewes, no one much notices that this area hasn't changed much from what it probably looked like three hundred years ago.

But if you take the old road, Delaware Route 9, you wander through the back country and are only likely to meet duck hunters. At one point, with a lake to one side and the river on the other, a watch tower has been erected for bird watchers and the like. It's very beautiful there, and quiet.

So one day I drove up, parked my car at the base of the tower, and climbed a hundred steps to the top. Blackbeard was not in evidence, but it was easy to see how he might feel pretty secluded in the coves and behind the trees. There were lots and lots of birds, interesting enough but mostly unidentifiable by me. Like most big-city

Copperhead

lovers of the environment, I mostly classify birds as little brown jobs (LBJ) and big black buggers (BBB). And then a car drove up, with some chattering teenagers.

From a hundred feet up, it was hard to tell what they were saying, and it probably didn't matter much. Until suddenly one of the girls screeched out, "Oh look! There's a big snake under that man's car! "

One of the boys in the car shouted out, "That's a copperhead snake! I've never seen one so big!"

And so, they roared off into the distance, leaving the marshy paradise to me and the snake. What do I do now?

I waited, hoping the snake would go away. But it started to get dark, and now it was even more unattractive to chase around with snakes. So, creeping to the bottom of the stairs, I made a dash for the car door, jumped in, and slammed it tight.

As I drove away, I could not see any snake on the ground under the place where I had parked. To this day, I don't know if there really was a snake there or not.

TOPIC 384 Right Angle Club 2017 => BLOG 3712 The Zimmerman Telegram

The Zimmerman Telegram

Arthur Zimmermann

Millions died because of one stolen telegram.

Some time in February, 1917, Zimmerman the German foreign minister sent a telegram to the President of Mexico, in code. The Germans sensed their submarine warfare might win the war for them, he wrote, and so it might be very helpful to have a second front attack the allies' main supplier, the United States. Germany would then win World War I, able to give Mexico --Texas, New Mexico and Arizona. The British intercepted the telegram, decoded it, and wasted no time putting the translation on Woodrow Wilson's desk.

Wilson had just won a Presidential election on the platform, "He kept us out of war." Furthermore, the Germans were the single largest ethnic minority in America. But no matter. Nevertheless, within a few days, Wilson stood before a joint meeting of Congress and urged them to declare war on Germany.

Annual Report 2017

Telegram in Code

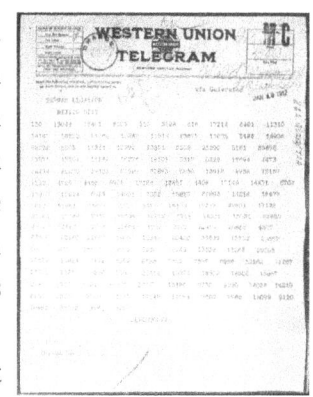

The consequences were immediate: the German minority was cowed with shame, and counting World War II as a continuation of World War I, sixty million people were killed. Because of a single heedless telegram. In retrospect, Wilson should have kept it quiet, privately negotiating something from Germany in return for ignoring the affront, and maybe keeping us out of both World wars. That's the sort of thing that gets played around with, when a responsible leader creates an uproar over catching an enemy with red hands. Otherwise, the carelessness tempts diplomats to assume he really did want a war, and needed a pretext for it.

It may violate the Constitution or some partisan law created by Congress, but it's the way diplomacy has been conducted ever since--well, since Benjamin Franklin was Ambassador to France, at any rate. It isn't exactly leadership, but it might have saved millions of lives. Muhlenberg told us, "There's a time to preach, and a time to fight." What he forgot was the part about preaching.

TOPIC 384 Right Angle Club 2017 => BLOG 3701 Uncorking the Past

Uncorking the Past
New blog 2017-02-11 03:42:11 description

The Right Angle Club was recently visited by Patrick E. McGovern, PhD. Scientific Director, Biomolecular Archaeology Project, Adjunct Professor, Anthropology, University of Pennsylvania Museum of Anthropology and Anthropology. Author,"The Quest for Wine, Beer, and Other Alcoholic Beverages; "Rediscovering ancient fermented beverages throughout the world."

Professor McGovern calculates that alcohol has been used as an intoxicating beverage for over 2700 years. Because our species began in Africa, that's the place you first find evidence of booze. As a matter of fact, the

Patrick E. McGovern PhD

7

Milky Way is just filled with loose alcohol, with millions of gallons floating around its center, so alcohol has probably been around for eons longer than we know. Alcohol is just a step of fermentation away from sugar, so it has probably been bubbling around almost as long as life.

The association of yeast fermentation with cell life has fascinated at least one other Penn Professor (Doug Wallace), who feels mitochondria are pieces of plants which have somehow got incorporated into animal cells, and probably account for the limited carbohydrate metabolism in animal forms, concentrating an unusually large proportion of cancer transformations in the process. If so, it's a mixture of good and evil, like so much of life.

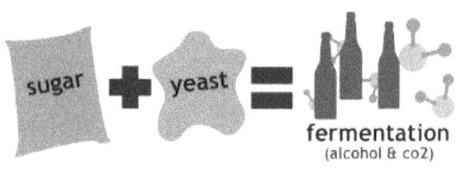

Alcohol Fermentation

So if it's so easy to transform carbohydrate into alcohol, it figures, the dominant beverage will be a fermentation of the local dominant carbohydrate. For the most part that's rice in the Orient (beer), fruit in central Asia (wine), and a tribe's favorite beverage tends to endure as long as they stay in the same region, eating the same food. I was tempted to ask about the beer-wine divide along the Rhine River, but decided not to veer too far from archaeology or chemistry. The spread of potato-generated vodka seemed abstraction enough for the lunch-time entertainment of gentlemen who do lunch together, ride the train together, and occasionally venture into off-color jokes and games of chance.

We did sample Dr. McGovern's own private stock, a mixture of wine, beer and mead. Quite tasty.

TOPIC 384 Right Angle Club 2017 => BLOG 3730 The Wistars Think Big, But Talk Softly

The Wistars Think Big, But Talk Softly

The closer the object is to the microscope, the shorter the focal length will be.

The Wistar Institute sits on the Penn campus, surrounded by Penn buildings. But it is entirely independent of Penn, dedicated to doing cutting-edge research which leads to practical applications later. They have fourteen new laboratories dedicated to fields most people know nothing about, and lots of old laboratories dedicated to the same. It's certainly something to have a scientific institute in our midst, especially one which refrains from blowing its own horn, and yet privately regards anything short of a Nobel Prize, as a failure.

A recent speaker at the Right Angle Club was James Hayden, the Managing Director of Wistar's Imaging Facility. His specialty seems to be taking pictures through a microscope, which conform to the general principle that the closer the image is to the microscope, the shorter the focal distance must become. The consequence is that microscopic pictures are unable to see all the way through the entire slice at any one focal length wider than the cell itself. The advent of digital photography requires a full thickness slice, but only a portion of its depth is visible at any one time and must be stained. Gradually the impression emerges that full-depth digital photography requires a three-dimensional scale. If time is a fourth dimension, there are two more dimensions to round out the six dimensions which are photographed by a million-dollar microscope. And the resulting image, of which he showed many, stops resembling a pea in a pod with smooth edges, and increasingly looks like a network of bushy strands with a nucleus buried deep within its depths.

The Wistar Institute

James Hayden

He described one extreme of this process as coming from boring a hole in the top of a mouse's skull, replacing the hole with a small window of glass, and showing a single melanoma cell metastasizing through the mouse's brain like a sheaf of wheat invading a cornfield. The heat it requires to keep the cell alive is often enough to damage the region, and all sorts of technical problems emerge from staining the cell part with pretty, but toxic, dyes. Having looked at a great many tissue slices after they were "fixed" (ie killed) by soaking in chemicals, I can tell you the old style looks nothing like the new one. It's going to take a long time and a lot of money to use this higher resolution, but you can tell at a glance that our thought processes about what cells are doing, will undergo some radical changes in the near future. And it will require a lot more expensive research to determine whether these new insights will be worth the money. Let's hope they are.

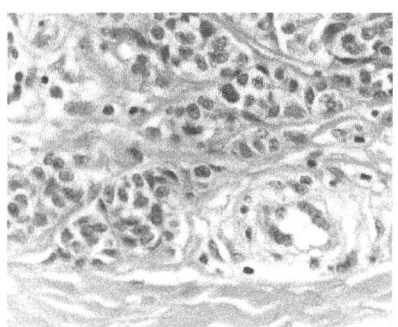

Melanoma Cell

Mr. Hayden promised to look into whether it might be possible to send an Internet link to a multi-dimensional picture of a cell in action, in which case members of the Right Angle club may be able to see this wonder in the original. Otherwise, it's sort of like Galileo's telescope, forcing the sceptic to take the inventor's word for it, as the only alternative to burning at the stake. In that particular historical case, the Pope was unable to decide which to do, so as I remember it he banished the guy.

Galileo›s telescope

Right Angle Club

TOPIC 384 Right Angle Club 2017 => BLOG 3698 The Burdens of the Rich

The Burdens of the Rich

Pulitzer Prize

The details are hazy, but sometime after graduating as a Registered Nurse my mother-in-law had a spell as a private-duty nurse for the daughter of Mrs. Pulitzer, and, I suppose later, became head nurse in the University of Pennsylvania unit in France, during World War I. Let's talk about Mrs. Moore, first. The Pulitzers had given the Pulitzer Prize, owned a chain of newspapers, and naturally owned several houses. Although I have to imagine there was a Mr. Moore somewhere, everything was referred to as if it belonged to Mrs. Moore, and Mr. Moore never appeared in the stories. They had a child with rheumatic fever, who was the reason they had a private nurse. Mrs. Moore devoted one afternoon a week to paying bills, which were numerous because of all the staff they employed at several houses scattered around the country, in New York, at Bar Harbor, and so on. One day, seated at her desk, she turned to the nurse, and asked her if she had any idea what a burden it all was.

My mother-in-law had always been very self-assured, and this time she drew herself up in full nurse dignity. "Mrs. Moore," she said, "I don't feel a bit sorry for you." But as more than a century goes past, I have come to see the rich lady had a point. What purpose is there to being rich, if you are expected to spend large amounts of time being a clerk? There were diamonds and minks to be got out of storage for the banquets, and then put away with moth crystals. There were silver spoons to be counted, and portraits of ancestors to be varnished. The gardener seemed to dipping into the best wine, the kitchen maid didn't clean up properly, the roof in the Florida house leaked. Instead of being the rich lady with a glamorous life, she was at best acting the part of mayor of a small town. And instead of being awestruck, her hired nurse was in effect telling her she was a spoiled brat. The story dramatizes, to be the head nurse of a famous hospital, helping the doughboys win the war to end all wars, that was somebody to look up to.

Miss Brothers (Ms. Miriam Blakely)

It wasn't the work. Anyone who has watched nurses rebel against typewriters in one generation and sit glued to a monitor with a very similar keyboard in the computerized phase of change, can recognize it wasn't the work. Not even if it means picking bloody sponges off the operating room floor, or the final degradation of digging out an impaction with others watching you do it. The hallmark, the final test, was to do it without hesitation, and never display the slightest sign of complaint. Because the point of pride was to be useful without the slightest sign of disgust. Dignity, doing something which other girls recoiled at doing. The snotty little brats.

It took some time for me to recognize that the image of nursing was formed in Nursing School, so strongly that the Nursing School was really the heart of any hospital. They would come back to reunions for generations, regaling their old friends with stories of Miss This or That, the tough old head nurse with a heart of gold. The head nurse was the mother-figure, and the role model. Anything you could do, she could do better. When she dismissed you, you deserved to be dismissed. You didn't know starch until you saw her starched uniform. And cap. You could tell what school had trained her, after a glance at her cap. And when the caps went, the uniforms were replaced with green un-ironed operating room gowns, not the same thing, at all. The schools were replaced by money from the US Government, sought after by the nursing lobby, and eagerly accepted by the administrators of hospitals, who didn't know what they were doing. The girls didn't know any better, either, thinking what they needed was a diploma. So now we contemplate a nurse with a bachelor's degree, or even a doctorate, without the faintest idea what to do, placed in charge of practical nurses in their forties who know everything about nursing worth knowing. So they retreat into the nurse's lounge, writing volumes of notes which no one ever reads. The girls who enter the few schools left are much the same. Show me a well-run hospital and I'll show you a hospital that still has a school. Show me a hospital that recruits its nurses from a near-by university, and I'll show you a hospital which is run by administrators.

Nursing School

TOPIC 384 Right Angle Club 2017 => BLOG 3711 Ethnic Cemeteries

Ethnic Cemeteries

Ed Snyder

Schneider, spelled Snyder (or Snider) is almost certainly a Pennsylvania Dutch surname in some sense. So I presume Ed Snyder is of that derivation, but at any rate he addressed the Right Angle Club recently

Meeting House on 4th

on the subject of photographing cemeteries. Along the way, he seems to have picked up a lot of historical facts about graveyards, which he put together into a fascinating story. I get the impression that many of the traditions he described had their origin in Europe and were transported here by various waves of immigration, so we don't have much information about the origins of the customs, except by inference.

The Quakers who settled Philadelphia in the early 1680's didn't believe in putting your name or your picture on anything, saying that was idolatry. That, plus the yellow fever epidemics, accounts for the fact that the Meeting House at Fourth and Arch has forty thousand people buried in its yard, in five layers, but only has two tombstones. Just why those two were exceptions is not described. Jonathan E. Rhoads, the famous University of Penn surgeon, has his name on a pavilion there, to which he raised loud objection, but finally died there himself, saying, "It didn't look so bad." So we have comparatively few early Quaker monuments still standing in the Quaker City, although it seems pretty certain the Quakers are not responsible for the midnight vandalism now sweeping the country, toppling tombstones. In any event, there definitely is an anti-cemetery movement going around in our nation, possibly dating back to the days when bodies of parishioners were buried in churchyards if they were in good standing, sort of like a giant compost heap. On the other hand, some people remember that Antigone went to some lengths to recover and honor her dead brother on the battle-field of ancient Greece. And that one of the reasons the Romans fed the early Christians to the lions was their horror at the retention of the bones

Laurel Hill Cemeteries

of ancestors in the catacombs, actually taking residence in the mortuaries in the expectation of a second coming for everybody. The Mormon infatuation with genetic ancestors may be part of this idea.

It has been said that if you stick a shovel in the ground anywhere, you will encounter a cemetery, but not in Philadelphia. Somewhere around 1830 we imported the French set of traditions of cemeteries, which you can still see as the questionable tombstones of Abelard and Heloise outside Paris. Laurel Hill in Philadelphia was started as an intentional commercial imitation, at a time when you had to take a boat on the Schuylkill to get there, taking the whole family along to have an all-day picnic among your ancestors; and mighty industrial potentate families competed to construct the biggest most expensive mausoleum for the family. Laurel Hill has since fallen into some disrepair, but there is a restoration movement actively repairing it, collecting donations, tracing histories, etc. Neill Bringhurst, a former president of the Right Angle Club, was once the owner, but he vigorously disliked the whole idea and sold it. Woodland, near the University of Pennsylvania is the other surviving cemetery of this elegance, and it is kept up much better than Laurel Hill, except for the tangled bushes around the periphery to maintain privacy. Woodland is right next to an extensive trolley-car terminal, thus conveying some idea of its former popularity. Prior to being a cemetery, it was the mansion site of Andrew Hamilton,

Marble Angels

whom George Washington used to visit on his way to Mount Vernon. As you recall, this Hamilton was the original Philadelphia Lawyer, who went to New York to defend the freedom of speech of Peter Zenger the newspaper man accused of telling the truth when he slandered the Governor. Considering the successor governors of New York, it's a good thing he won the case. History has it he was a young unrecognized lawyer, but in fact Hamilton was the most eminent lawyer of his time, having originally purchased what is now Independence Hall.

The traditions of marble angels hovering over tombstones seems to have been imported by Irish and Italian immigrants, and is reflected in their present cemeteries. And the Pennsylvania Dutch tombstones and records are intact in Hummelstown PA, dating back to the Seventeenth century. It reflects that this particular branch landed in New York, went up the Hudson to Kingston, and back down to the Harrisburg area on the Susquehanna. Meanwhile, the Quakers further East were burying their dead in layers without "markers".

There's probably a lot more to this history, but burials are sort of private affairs, and most church groups are unaware of the dissenting attitudes, not very far away.

TOPIC 384 Right Angle Club 2017 => BLOG 3713 Deputy Managing Director

Deputy Managing Director

Judge Benjamin Lerner

The Deputy Managing Director of Philadelphia, former Judge Benjamin Lerner, honored the Right Angle Club by coming to lunch, recently. He immediately improved our opinion of him by first explaining why he resigned as Judge.

It seems the Inside Baseball of the last Mayor's election shifted the politics quite a lot. Under Mayor Nutter, the department heads reported to the Mayor, but under the new Mayor Kenney, everybody reported to the Managing Director. So Judge Lerner promptly resigned his judgeship and became Deputy Managing Director, if you see the drift of the power shift. He had become exercised about the drug problem in Philadelphia, wanted to do something, and knew the ropes to get it done. You've got to like a man like that.

Drug Situation

It doesn't matter what got him mad. The drug situation in this town is a disgrace, and any number of reasons might have got the Judge angry. It's too early to know what he can accomplish in his short time in office, but I have every confidence that if he can't improve things, it's time for all of us to move to another city. Because no one can fix it if he can't.

In fact, I happen to know something he admitted he didn't know. Several years ago I was mugged in the middle of a police stake-out, so they caught the culprit. That's a pretty open and shut case, but the defense attorney apparently tried to stall me out of being a witness. For nine --nine -- consecutive trials, I cancelled my appointments and appeared at 9 AM. By the afternoon, I sat there waiting to be told the trial was postponed, for a prisoner in custody, no less. In any event, I watched nearly a hundred trials during this period, and every one of the defendants told the Judge he had been smoking drugs, outside the courtroom in the corridor. Well, as a witness I was free to walk around, and I can tell you nobody was smoking drugs in the corridor. I knew for a fact they were telling the judge they were addicts, when they weren't. I haven't the slightest idea why they were doing this, but I presume they had discovered some loophole in the law, and were exploiting it. The rule that drug addicts escape a jury trial might be a plausible explanation, but I simply don't know.

The Judge agreed with me he had no idea of this behavior, or if it continued to happen. But I am willing to bet, it's now going to stop.

TOPIC 384 Right Angle Club 2017 => BLOG 3714 Suited To A "T"

Suited To A "T"

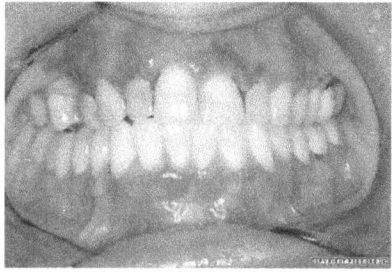

Mucous Membrane Pemphigoid

After sixty years as a doctor, it's a little disconcerting to find I have a disease I never heard of. It's better in a way, but in this sense it is worse, to be cured by a treatment I never heard of, either. The disease is mucous membrane pemphigoid, and the cure is Rituxamide. Am I right? Most readers have never heard of either one, but like just about every other patient, I think you all must just be panting to hear about it.

It turns out I had heard about the disease, but it had changed its name from lichen planus to mucous membrane pemphigoid. The drug, Rituximab, has been around since 1997, treating rheumatoid arthritis, so it's not completely novel, either. When we got these semantic issues straightened out, and I had experienced a second round of treatment, I attended a seminar on lung cancer. That's the sort of thing doctors do for entertainment.

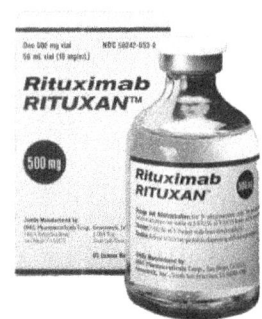

Rituximab

To my puzzlement, I was told a "me, too" variant of this drug extended the life of lung cancer patients, but only if they were heavy smokers who quit smoking. That sounded sort of funny, very much like saying you live longer from lung cancer if you smoke heavily and don't quit. So, you get a little euphoric when you take a steroid drug to ease the Rituximab, so I was overcome with audacity to go to the microphone and announce I thought they lived longer, not because it helped the lung cancer, but because they had fewer heart attacks and strokes from the smoking they had quit. Of course, I was politely told I didn't know what I was talking about. But an immunologist in the audience rose to say he agreed with me, because he had been giving the drug to practically every patient in his immunology practice, and quite a few of them got better. (To explain, the drug knocks out the T cells, which mediate most autoimmune diseases, so it sounded plausible.) So that's where matters stand. And after everybody scrambles to try the drug on various autoimmune patients, some sort of order will probably emerge.)

But before everyone who reads this demands that his doctor give him this drug for itchy skin, let me tell you another story. My insurance company sent me what is known as an "EOB" (explanation of benefits) which had two numbers on it. In the upper left-hand corner, it said my bill was $67,000. In the lower right-hand corner, it said, the amount owed, was $0.00. Somewhere between the two numbers is the amount you would have to pay if you didn't have insurance, the rest is someone's mark-up. So, I set about to find out how much the drug really costs to manufacture, and I don't yet know. Someone said $4, but I can scarcely believe it.

TOPIC 384 Right Angle Club 2017 => BLOG 3717 Post-Graduate Medical Education in Philadelphia

Post-Graduate Medical Education in Philadelphia

Lawyers will tell you a newly graduated lawyer doesn't know much about the practical aspects of law practice. That seems to date back to the days when a lawyer didn't go to law school at all, but instead studied the law in the office of a practicing lawyer. It seemed to work out all right, since Abraham Lincoln didn't go to law school, and the last Supreme Court Justice not to go to law school was "Scoop" Jackson, who presided over the Nuremberg Trials. The first law school in America was naturally at the University of Pennsylvania, founded by a lawyer who was very influential at the Constitutional Convention, also held in Philadelphia -- James Wilson,

Robert H. Jackson

so all those lawyers who wrote the Constitution had either studied law without benefit of Law school, or else were rich and had travelled to London to study at the Inns of Court. James Wilson had a famous battle at his house at 3rd and Walnut, subsequently known as the Battle of Fort Wilson, where five later delegates to the Constitutional convention were attacked by what some call a "mob" in 1779, and probably carried a vivid recollection of the event when they were later writing the "original intent" of that document. In any event, the five law schools which style themselves "national law schools" and from which almost all of the big law firms draw corporate lawyers, are pretty firm about the fact that they will teach the associates all they need to know about the practicalities of the law. There are dozens of "state law schools" who feel differently about this, but it can be noticed that all of the Supreme Court Justices come from national law schools at the present time.

Well, medical schools were pretty much divided along the same lines until the Flexner report of 1913, and subsequently the division was between general practitioners and specialists, with the specialists receiving practical training as residents in hospitals. The medical school administrators never liked this arrangement, and have worked hard to envelop specialty training into the school hospitals. If you hear talk of "town and gown", this is the topic they are usually centered on. The division was pretty static until 1965, held together by the fact that residents in training were paid very little or nothing, so the schools were restrained in their eagerness. With the advent of Medicare, however, arrangements resulted in -- for practical purposes -- the residents being paid a generous salary in order to pay off their medical school debts. Nobody has mentioned this evolution in the current Obamacare-Trumpcare squabble because it isn't central to the argument, but it's part of the mix, all right. Obamacare went a considerable distance toward centralizing specialist training in the payment juggling, and before that, it had a lot to do with Medicare retaining open teaching wards, when the clear intent was promised to start at the economic bottom of the ladder with semi-private accommodations for everyone. And it had a lot to do with the closing of Philadelphia General Hospital, which had seven thousand beds during the Civil War, and three thousand at the end of World War II. One post-war blue ribbon committee, convened to evaluate PGH, began its report with "Philadelphia can indeed be proud..." At the end of WWII, sixty-five percent of the Delaware Valley hospital beds, in 165 hospitals, were free ward beds.

Abraham Flexner

On the other hand, it must be admitted that thirty years has been added to average American life expectancy, in the past century. The system can't be terribly bad, although it is a trifle expensive, and every surviving hospital has a brand-new hospital building, plus more administrators than doctors, depending on how you define an administrator, or a doctor for that matter.

To get back to "continuing" post-graduate medical education, both the College of Physicians and the County Medical Society have largely given it up, replaced in part by seminars financed by drug firms. Naturally, these seminars favored the use of the latest drug, were featured with free lunches for the residents, and highly criticised for a conflict of interest. So in time Sydney Kimmel the

College of Physicians of Philadelphia

philanthropist was persuaded that continuing medical education (at a time of almost tumultuous innovation) was in a sorry state in Philadelphia, and donated something like $250 million to the establishment of a medical school that would do nothing else, or words to that effect. I attend six or so all-day seminars yearly, and find them to be excellent. The last one only cost me $190, and the drug companies donated the meals. So the reviews have to be mixed, since I keep wondering where all of the rest of the money went, and keep thinking about that aphorism of Hippocrates, which speaks of teaching without charge.

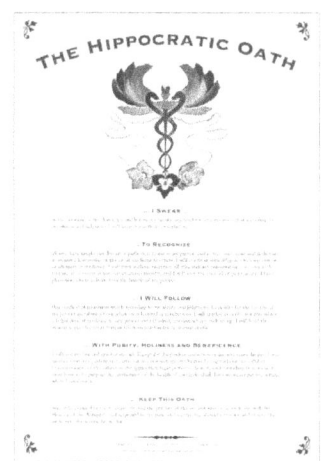

Hippocratic Oath

As historical background, the following exerpt is taken from the original Hippocratic Oath: *To hold him who has taught me this art as equal to my parents and to live my life in partnership with him, and if he is in need of money to give him a share of mine, and to regard his offspring as equal to my brothers in male lineage and to teach them this art - if they desire to learn it -* **without fee and covenant**; *to give a share of precepts and oral instruction and all the other learning to my sons and to the sons of him who has instructed me and to pupils who have signed the covenant and have taken an oath* **according to the medical law, but no one else.**

The modernized Hippocratic Oath, written by Louis Lasagna of Tufts University, goes as follows: *I swear to fulfill, to the best of my ability and judgment, this covenant: I will respect the hard-won scientific gains of those physicians in whose steps I walk, and* **gladly share such knowledge as is mine with those who are to follow.**

TOPIC 384 Right Angle Club 2017 => BLOG 3727 (1) Medicine at the Two Ends of Life: First year of Life, and Last Years of Life.

(1) Medicine at the Two Ends of Life: First year of Life, and Last Years of Life.

Every person is born and will die. For other health care, a cure might be possible.

Benjamin Franklin founded the Ivy League's University of Pennsylvania, but he was surely no academic. He was a practical man, looking for practical results, and some of the fiercest battles he fought concerned the direction and purposes of his University, especially the nature of its mission. At a time when most Ivy League Universities were mostly divinity schools, he would not nnsylvaniatolerate it that way for his own, and to this day the University of Pennsylvania has no divinity school, although it does have something very close. If there had been such a thing in his day as a Nobel Prize, he would have won it for his achievements in electricity. In the centuries-long journey from divinity school to occupational credentials, Franklin's position and the general academic position have drawn marginally closer together. The first academic course in science was only taught around the time of the Civil War. The term "philosophy" would now be used as a word for "science", and a Doctorate of Nuclear Physics would puzzle most physics majors, even though they aspire to achieve that Ph.D. degree. The American Philosophical Society is quite definitely a scientific society, and most definitely was founded by Benjamin Franklin. These were not idle arguments in the Age of Reason.

To speak more practically, a great bulk of scientific achievement consists of experiments to reduce complexity, and ultimately to reduce costs. No doubt there are scientific discoveries of new fields, and probably the greatest prestige attaches to those who uncover some totally original feature. But the surprising bulk of the effort is devoted to simplifying and reducing costs. If a scientist employed by a big company should discover some cheaper way to do something more simply, he will be rewarded, and it may well make his career. If he discovers how to solve a mathematical equation in significantly fewer steps, his accomplishment is described as "elegant". That's the nature of science, to accomplish a goal, no matter how complicated. To make it profitable, you cut out a lot of the fumbling and get right down to the nub of a solution, with fewer steps, and cheaper materials. If you are unsatisfied with this generalization, just compare some random salaries of chemical engineers, with theoretical chemists.

There's even a story they tell in England about Franklin and King George. It seems lightning struck the steeple of St. Paul's Cathedral, and quite naturally the King consulted with Franklin about a lightning rod since Franklin lived a few blocks away. The King wanted a brass ball on the top of his church. Franklin made the rare miscalculation of openly disagreeing with the King. "No, your Majesty, it should be an iron spike. " The English imply the story depicts a foreign printer telling the King what to do and was, therefore, himself a fool. The American version of the same story would have it the King was a fool to tell the greatest living expert on lightning rods what was what about lightning rods. The founder of the American diplomatic corps probably would never have chosen such words, but "Who the hell do you think you are, telling *me* what is best in lightning rods", would probably summarize it. Well, America and Great Britain fought an eight-year revolution over this difference in attitudes, and so it seems likely Franklin and the Trustees of the University he founded, used stronger words than are now reported in alumni magazines.

The moral of all this is, no matter how silly the argument seems to strangers, the protagonists sometimes feel strongly enough to make trouble for those who do not accord their views a proper deference. The fact Franklin acted in such an out-of-character way, is probably proof of how strongly he really felt about it.

So, to sum it all up, it is an American trait to acknowledge start-up costs, but to surmise that in the long run, it's cheaper to eliminate a disease than to count the cost of curing it. No one knows whether research will lead to eliminating the cost of disease, but most Americans will presume it will, and most Americans will somewhat minimize the time it will take to accomplish it. We imitate the attitudes we suppose our mentor must have had, and indeed he may well have had them. The logic of the matter will only take you so far. At the rate we are going, I feel we might eliminate most diseases within the span of the next century. I feel medical costs a century from now will be -- not just could be --eliminated except for the cost of childbirth and death. You may disagree; no one knows. That's why participation in a long-term program to deal with the matter, should remain voluntary until the outcome is clear. In matters like this, everyone tends to overstate his case. Therefore, no one is entitled to force others to swallow their doubts.

(2) Death as a Portion of Lifetime Health Expense

No one asks to be born, but once born, there will be an unavoidable additional cost for dying. No amount of scientific research can eliminate the twin cost of being born, and of dying. Nations differ about such costs, but if you want to know what they should be, just look at what they are. Such irreducible healthcare costs are about half of the present total. That leaves the other half of the cost, which might be eliminated by scientific research. If it takes a century to do it, total elimination of disease cost might be accomplished at a price of about a half a percent per year. That's not totally impossible.

But scientific healthcare cost is different from truck maintenance, in part because some of the components cannot be replaced. The cost of prolonging useful truck life is largely the cost of devising improved maintenance; it's the best we can do within remaining mindful of what it costs. What's mainly different from healthcare is we have declared an end to economic ("useful") life at the time of retirement. Unless productivity of the elderly starts to improve, their retirement costs will rise, even if the cost of healthcare approaches zero. Let's put it another way: the faster healthcare costs come down, the faster retirement costs will go up. Simple arithmetic shows real healthcare costs can only be further reduced by half, or $175,000 per lifetime. Useful lifetimes, on the other hand, have already been declared finished by the age of 60-65. The gap is still widening, but even if research stops that trend, things will get worse. Using actuarial methods, it has been calculated that average lifetime medical costs are now about $350,000 per individual, *denominated in year 2000 dollars*, and assuming present longevity. That doesn't count health insurance cost, by the way. And it doesn't help to say Social Security payments should be progressively raised, because that's also incomplete arithmetic. Old folks must find something remunerative to do.

With some reservations, the Medicare agency calculates half its expense is devoted to the last four years of someone's life, all of its present expense is approximately $50 billion annually. Unfortunately, 9 million Medicare recipients are disabled but not yet aged 65, so terminal care costs less than $143,000 per person in year 2000 dollars, if you include many permanently disabled persons. Reversing the calculation, you might save $200,000 per person if you paid for nothing but terminal care. Additionally paying for childbirth and neonatal costs might still reduce average savings to approximately $175,000, or about half. That's approximately how you might justify the slogan, "Paying for only the essential two ends of life, would likely cut government costs in half." Another way of looking at it would be to accept Mrs. Sibelius's approximation that half of Medicare costs are borrowed. Paying only for birth and death would leave the present system roughly intact, except it would eliminate the borrowing. Better hurry up, interest rates are expected to rise.

Leaving things roughly intact would assume research costs are lumped with treatment costs. Both offsetting costs might be projected to disappear in a century, although probably at variable speeds. Furthermore, providers of treatment and providers of research are only human; they tend to attack the most expensive diseases first, particularly focusing on painful and mortal conditions . That's only a rough approximation. Everybody has lobbyists, and Congress must take care to balance inputs against the goal: to reduce the net sum of research costs and treatment costs in year 2000 dollars, by a fraction of a percent (?half a percent?) per year, and to keep that up for a century.

It doesn't sound impossible to construct and enforce such a budget on the combined treatment and research communities, even recognizing the vagaries of taxation and demography. Perhaps a five-year running average would be manageable. But there is one big thing missing. We swept this issue under the rug for fifty years and we could do it for another fifty, if we tried hard enough. That is -- we have neglected to consider the cost of success. As the health of the public improves, they live longer. In our system, that means they will need more money for retirement. Lots of money.

With a fixed retirement age, things get worse. Someone is currently running for President of France on a platform of *lowering* the retirement age to 55. We are, by contrast, at least grudgingly raising the retirement age to 67, at the risk of tearing the political parties apart attempting it. Although Medicare is technically an amendment of the Social Security Act, the retirement age of Social Security has remained essentially stationary, while benefits rise slowly but menacingly in response to inflation at 3% a year. Retirement costs are almost certain to rise more quickly than health costs fall, because illnesses are episodic whereas retirement is continuous. Aside from the impossibility of negotiating a solution to this monetary quandary, there is the social disruption of having nothing remunerative to do. There is only so much golf or bridge a normal person can stand to do. Only so much traveling to do before you meet yourself coming back. Only so many fish to catch, entertaining to do, and booze to drink. We have some serious thinking to do, before we find anything which is as satisfying as having an occupation. Young people imagine taking a vacation from age 18 to 48 is the same as from ages 60 to 90, but it isn't the same at all. Let's repeat: the cost of improved medical care is not primarily that the doctors will fail, it is that the doctors may succeed, and then you won't know what to do with yourself.

TOPIC 384 Right Angle Club 2017 => BLOG 3722 Two Central Mistakes In The Design of Health Insurance.

Two Central Mistakes In The Design of Health Insurance

Concentrate on two flaws in healthcare. If uncorrected, no scoring -- dynamic or otherwise -- will conceal collective failure to address health costs seriously. Other problems should stand aside while these two are considered.

The first is pay-as-you-go. Its name misleads, because the younger generation, enjoying good health, pays its parent's high health costs toward the end of life, passing their own to their children. Medicare's first generation thus was given a free ride, so my mother who died at the age of 103, represents a whole generation who paid essentially nothing for thirty years of expenses. This example of debt being passed along for fifty years, got bigger with time throughout 18% of Gross Domestic Product , even with low interest rates. We must liquidate that debt, invest the idle savings until needed for healthcare, and eliminate the annual 50% Medicare deficit to creditors. Quite a task.

An important result would be the incentive to save, replacing the incentive to spend. HSAs demonstrate net savings in health- cost of at least 20%, because in a Health Savings Account, young people of each generation **earn interest while they save for their own subsequent health costs, instead of spending immediately for anonymous demographic groups of strangers.** At this point, another unexpected bonus appeared:

Some people have the luck not to get very sick, thus able to accumulate tax-exempt money in the account until they turn 66. Since everyone gets Medicare eventually, current law turns HSA accumulations into largely unnoticed tax-exempt retirement funds. (It's mandatory, whereas I would prefer an option.)

A second blunder reached the surface. Medicare provided better medical care, but made longevity increase, laying bare it had added thirty years of retirement cost. Sickness cost is episodic, but retirements are continuous. Consequently, additional retirement costs can become several times as costly as the sickness costs they replace. Talk about sweeping something under a rug.

It will not be easy to produce packages of proposals to cover the transition to a less costly funding system. But no health funding scheme other than Health Savings Accounts provides even the flimsiest scaffold for addressing this issue. Social Security has such a mission, but is hopelessly underfunded. So the second of two big problems facing us, is : we failed to anticipate success.

***

There is a third big elephant in this room to be wiped out with a paragraph of legislation. Scratch any regulation and you find a lobbyist underneath it. Half the population enjoys a tax deduction denied the other half, and that other half is restless. Unless big corporations yield to the demand for equality, there will be continued agitation. No doubt lobbyists promise to address this issue under tax reform, and perhaps plan to reserve their concessions for later trade-offs. But one half of the public owes such a large debt to that other half, little *quid pro quo* is justified. Permitting HSA to pay the premiums for required high-deductible insurance could accomplish it in a handful of sentences.

The fourth big issue offers hope, instead of despair. Medicare coverage for young unemployable persons ("disabled") was effectively broadened to over 90% , by unemployed effectively changed to unemployable. Higher costs were thus added to basic costs for 9 million of the 46 million regular Medicare recipients, rather than remaining lumped with the 30 million uninsured unemployables (requiring specialized programs.) These higher costs of average Medicare per employable person, have been overlooked by most commentators, making ordinary Medicare seem costlier than it really is. It's bad, all right, but not quite as bad as it seems. Documenting that fact, as well as shifting the medical income tax inequity to the tax bill, leaves only **two new issues to address: pay-as-you-go, and retirement funding.** That›s quite enough for a first round.

Paying for Medicare Transition with Trust Funds

Since Medicare finance isn't affected by the Affordable Care Act, there's a short-term temptation to forget it. But its deficits and poor design are at the heart of the Medicare problem, and persist in its decendants. At the end of this short book, the reader will realize it covers lifetime health insurance, except it left a big hole in the middle. Obamacare can only be absorbed after we see how much of it will survive, and uncover what it really costs.

Since its finance isn't much affected by the Affordable Care Act, there's a temptation to skip over Medicare. But ACA deficits and design flaws frequently grew out of Medicare's initial design decisions. Furthermore, the scientific tendency has been to cure acute diseases of younger people first, so the trend predicts still more high expense (chronic disease) patients will migrate toward Medicare. The ultimate prediction is for little to be left uncured at some distant time, except in the first year of life and the last year of life.

Changed Circumstances. There have been three main changes since some wag called Medicare the third rail of politics -- "just touch it and you're dead". The first change since 1965 is *much-increased longevity* as a consequence of much-better healthcare. Someone must have seen this coming, but apparently no one spoke up. Although prolonged retirement is expensive, notice also how it prolongs the period of time available for compound interest to work, so the income curve starts to bend upward after thirty or forty years, regardless of the economy.

Secondly, *passive, or index, investing has greatly simplified and strengthened amateur investing*. Finally, the *Health Savings Accounts appeared, often producing savings of 20-30%*. It›s time to re-examine the assumptions of 1965, with these three lights shining on them: longevity, passive investing, and payment design. We are not recommending that HSA be entirely funded by index funds, but merely recoiling from too much debt backed by government guarantees.(see below)

Proposed. In "Ye Olde" Medicare, the average beneficiary pays $56,000 per lifetime (in payroll withholding tax and premiums), but it actually costs the government at least $112,000 per person -- the remaining $50,000 or so per person is secondarily borrowed, so there are no left-overs for retirement. But prolonged longevity and longer retirement, hence more borrowing, are inevitable consequences of better healthcare with the present design. Viewed in that light, Medicare is broke. But viewed as a transition problem, it paradoxically addresses half of it; since half the Medicare transition is already covered by bond issues. Put that together with the halving provided by Last Year of Life re-insurance, and you have made big progress toward transition. We also offer several other proposals for transition.

Our "New" Medicare, by contrast, seemingly could pay for all its present medical care, plus appreciable retirement cost, with the same revenue. Minimal extra government debt, no rationing or curtailment of service. It does it without changing major program elements; **this is a financial change, not a medical one**. It really does let you keep your own doctor, and doesn't tell him how to treat you, because it doesn't concern such things. Half of all medical expense is covered by Medicare. And we propose to fund half of that, plus all of obstetrical/pediatric care, with First and Last Years of Life Re-Insurance. Transition begins to look feasible if we can convince old folks with a fixed income to take a chance on it.

Tools Seemingly Available for Transition to the New System, But Presently Not Provided For in Law: (See below) 1) Scientific break-through cures which significantly reduce the cost of Medicare. 2) Gradual buy-ins for latecomers, which significantly reduce the buy-in cost for people well past 65 at the start. 3) Special Trust Fund Extension eligibilities after death or before childbirth. Compound interest doesn›t need the owner to be alive. 4) Delaying the Start of a Childhood Roll-Over. 5) Graduated Retirement as funding develops. All of these will be explained later, and the news is not all bad.

Extra Tools, Needed From Congress: "Change the destination" of Medicare›s Withholding Tax, and Premiums, so the same money, plus interest, ends up in the individual›s Health Savings Account, instead of Medicare. That›s in return for the subscriber agreeing to buy out Medicare at its mandatory onset, plus any other imposed conditions. There is one technicality: the tax exemption is currently distributed through the income tax system, while it should be added to the HSA, instead. Furthermore, if a considerable surplus (more than $100, say) from compound interest persists after withdrawals, the choice of buying out Medicare can be offered at its beginning age up to the perpetuity limit (on average, age 104), *disregarding whether the depositor is still alive or covered by a special successor trust fund*. Re-depositing in an HSA should make such contributions tax-exempt and earn compound interest (we hope, at 7%) in an **escrowed** sub-account which *bypasses current medical costs until it is time to use them* for Medicare. At least, escrowed in a way which cannot be diverted from Medicare use. Therefore, average payroll-withholding transforms from $28,000 ($700 yearly for forty years, taxable) into health care worth on average 18% more than that, or $825, because it's *before-tax*, and at 7% grows to $138,000 at age 65 (Try that out on your Internet compound interest calculator). That's what folks are paying right now, but including the tax exemption isn't as smooth as it could be. Don't forget the escrow feature, which keeps people from being their own worst enemies when other purchases compete for the single-purpose savings escrow.

Starting at any age before 66, it could then transform $1400 yearly Medicare premiums, *before tax, and thus really $1650* into 18% more for twenty more years, and also pays *tax-exempt interest*. (Most people will find they have to read this several times, because Health Savings Accounts are the only plan enjoying these particular features.) The **net effect of augmented income tax augmentation, compounded, is to transform $56,000 before tax, into $534,000 beforetax at age 84, the present life expectancy, not counting $112,000 borrowed by the government, which we hope they can eventually stop borrowing**. That doesn't sound like good arithmetic, but If you don't believe it is possible, just try it on one of the Internet's free compound interest calculators. (Furthermore, if an *afterdeath trust fund* is created to the limit of a legal perpetuity [one lifetime plus 21 years], the present expenditure would be subsequently transformed by compound interest into whatever $2,066,000 is worth at the time, we should hope amply providing for all of Medicare, plus some generous retirement without government borrowing. You won›t be surprised to find others think this is more than you will need. We will later suggest better ways to rearrange the same facts, but this summary contains the general idea in highly condensed form.

Although an accumulation of over $2 million per subscriber seems adequate for any normal purpose, it should be recognized that this figure only applies to someone who started saving from birth and waited 104 years to collect. Therefore it would only be a theoretical issue for a long time. A far more generous sum is possible earlier if the original purposes of payments are ignored, and the principle adopted that the largest contribution should begin earliest. That maneuver results in payments age 104 of $30,165,195.00 which would make most people giggle. The obstacle to overcome is the resistance stirred up by matching Medicare premiums to newborn children's HSAs. However, if the system needs more money, this is the place to get it. By adopting this principle, a $2 million fund is achieved at age 60 instead of 104, which eliminates the need to consider several other strategies, expenses and objections thereto, subsequent to a Medicare buyout. It would make an $18,000 grandchild gift seem trivial, and last year of life strategy unnecessary, for example.

Transition costs dominate the replacement of almost any health insurance, so let's restate the theory. A J-shaped cost curve forces a J-shaped revenue stream. When you switch systems, you must reverse the order, paying expensive existing ones first; and funding proves inadequate unless you can double it. If you could just manage, it would be possible to make partial cost savings you could boast of, but except for the Postmortem Trust Fund way you must pay double for all of it, or give up the attempt. By contrast, if you have at your disposal a large new source of credit like a postmortem Trust Fund, with an elastic retirement fund absorbing embarrassing surpluses, you can survive early misjudgments. Medicare could pay for its entire cost with compound interest on what subscribers now contribute, save for the fact it will have inadequate cash flow from people on their deathbeds. But if the death of the subscriber is ignored, the inflow of funds from surviving depositors could continue into postmortem trust funds of the decedents. At 7% return, extending the payments to the length of a perpetuity (21 years) would multiply its amount four times, reducing the problem to a quarter of where it started. The transition time is thereby considerable shortened. For transition purposes, it might be wise to create a contingency fund, of up to $250 at birth. But remember, the size of the gap in a lifetime plan can only be finally addressed after we see what is to become of the ACA (Obamacare). For the purposes of this book, we simply treat the ACA as if it were revenue-neutral, a somewhat unlikely forecast, but a completely understandable assumption.

TOPIC 384 Right Angle Club 2017 => BLOG 3759 Broad Brush

Broad Brush
One-page summary of lifetime Health Savings Accounts

Other Voices: Rethink Lifetime Health Finance

Barron's recently invited 1000-word summaries of radical change proposals. tg.donlan@barrons.com
Health insurance financing is a gigantic wealth transfer system. Politically, it is described as a transfer from rich to poor. But it really is a transfer from one age bracket (working people) to two non-working ones, children and retirees. Add thirty years of longevity by curing the diseases of one age group faster than another, and the balance between age and wealth distributions gets bent out of shape. Socially, it's dangerous. It gets even worse to base one-year casualty insurance on employment, tempting employers to dump a system which ends when employment does, patched together by tax incentives. Average employment duration is around three years, so almost every condition soon becomes a pre-existing one, whenever

employees lose their insurance. Insurance companies see what's coming, and cannot be blamed for getting out before it collapses.

More revenue would help, but existing sources are almost exhausted at 18% of GDP, while rapid change in health delivery would flirt with disaster. But one thing remains: using the idle money in pay/as/you/go to fund a transition matching a change in spending incentives, or even scientific research eventually eliminating disease. It would work with income returns of between 3-7%. Compound interest on money already collected would pay the deficit. Extension of the age limits on Health Savings Accounts would stop the borrowing, and trust funds would extend the compounding for 21 years past the average age of death upward, to the point it would far exceed the need for retirement funding through taxation or borrowing. Transfer of $4000 of each grandparent's HSA surplus (at death plus 21) to the HSA of one grandchild would add another 21 years to compounding downward, leaving several millions of dollars per person for retirement, curing a number of social turmoils in the process. That probably wouldn't happen completely, but a Medicare surplus rather than a deficit would allow any transition to be much speedier. The present 2.9% employment tax presently collected from working people would equal or exceed what is needed if compounded. Since the new fiscal limits would be enforced by the laws of mathematics, there would be far less temptation to spend it on battleships. Further extensions of longevity would increase revenue faster than inflation could undermine it. Essentially, it would be asked to match 104 years of compounding-- with what took 42 years to accumulate. There's plenty of slack if you try those simple numbers on a free compound interest calculator, found on everybody's Internet. A second chance to do what we should have done in the first place.

True, the necessary change in incentives would come from unifying three systems into one lifetime one, incentivized by noticing the remarkable savings already created by millions of Mid-Western subscribers to HSA. A few sentences of amendments to existing law should be all that Congress needs to struggle with, since these are existing programs. Whereas the R's need to see a single-payer system has become a single-saver system, the D's can save face by asserting they are the same thing.

George Ross Fisher MD 3 Haddon Avenue South Haddonfield, NJ, 08033 Cell 215-280-6625 office 856-427-6135 Email: grfisheriii@gmail.com

TOPIC 384 Right Angle Club 2017 => BLOG 3695 Currencies Owned by Nations, or by People?

Currencies Owned by Nations, or by People?

King Midas

Let's remember why this subject came up -- we essentially don't have a monetary standard, gold or anything else, although it seems likely a suitable monetary standard would lead to a better state of *economic* affairs. King Midas is thought to have invented the metallic-standard idea, and whether that is true or not, national currencies backed by gold are thousands of years old. No doubt, the Spanish galleon idea was a new slogan for an old idea which goes back at least as far as paper money. Consequently, people carried the gold coins around in purses, but still trusted the King to accumulate the gold and mint it into coins for them.

History shows that kings regularly abused this intermediary role, by shaving the coins and other forms of short-weighting them. Meanwhile, kings felt they needed to accumulate funds for wars and other national purposes, and controlling the currency was a needed revenue generator. But land was also used for aggressive national purposes, rewarding local chieftains for their loyalty, and substituting for the loan of mercenaries or other war materials. But when you give away land, you give away part of your kingdom, always a risky business. The more you think about history, the more convincing is the argument for gold, from the point of view of the king, if he is the middle-man. The argument for the individual citizen to surrender his gold to the King to parcel out to the citizens a second time, is a little less dispositive. People have always grumbled about taxes, and demanded more than protection in return for paying them. But pacifists have always resisted taxes disproportionately, arguing if we could become more peaceful, we might need less taxes. In a modern context, it is hard to imagine individual citizens making atom bombs, aircraft carriers and other means of winning wars. Less convincingly, the idea of a government using taxes to create state capitalism, has been a second-best argument for governments to expropriate individual wealth. If it works at all, it has not proved itself in two hundred years of trying. Nevertheless, this line of thinking probably enlists significant leftist opposition to individual possession of physical wealth.

Gold Coins

Although the idea has provoked angry discussion for centuries, it is likely the opposition of leftists and the uneasiness of rightists would at best limit support to winning the agreement of a bare majority of the rest, probably only under convulsive circumstances, and probably only to a partial degree. The prospect of individual wealth possession, without forcible physical defeat, must content itself with sharing possession of the monetary standard with the government, until a partial test of the idea shows it has such economic advantages to trade and to peace, that further resistance is futile. The concept may possess such power, but it must overcome what is at present an unconvincable opposition, and rest its case on unexpected success with creeping implementation.

Industrial Revolution

The closest historical test would be the international experience with Spanish pieces of eight during the age of piracy. We do not have adequate history to use this period as a dispositive example, but it is certainly true that government was weak on the high seas And that national currencies regained dominance afterwards when governments got stronger. It is also true the age of piracy was followed by the Industrial Revolution, or the Age of Enlightenment, or the French Revolution. A case could be made that any one of these consequences had roots in the Age of Piracy, but not a sufficiently powerful one to end debate. Here again, we must carry analysis as far as we can, but only expect to settle the question after experimentation with it. So, let's describe it more fully, to see where that gets us.

TOPIC 384 Right Angle Club 2017 => BLOG 3716 Uber and 215 Get A Cab

Uber and 215 Get A Cab
New blog 2017-03-19 13:31:47 description

Uber or Taxi

Uber is a taxicab company which has been around for a year or so, but has finally caught on in Philadelphia, exposing some of the more disconcerting facts of taxi medallions. It is rumored to be true that the fees collected for taxi monopolies often contribute half of some city's budgets, although of course that couldn't be true in Philadelphia. A taxicab company buys a medallion for each cab, indicating a right to operate a cab, and the taxi drivers will tell you their medallions cost several hundred thousand dollars apiece. Most taxi drivers don't own their cabs, so these reports may contain an element of grievance against the actual owners, or the city, or both. At any rate, what is being sold is a monopoly, and the fares they charge customers must recover it. So Uber entered the scene, and the customers have a certain amount of sympathy with them. Uber isn't a taxi owner, it's sort of a cab-summoning system, but to the customer it's hard to tell a difference. To the city, which is in the medallion-selling, or perhaps monopoly pay-to-play business, it's an important legal distinction, which so far they haven't found a way to throttle. In the long run, of course, an improved and cheaper cab-summoning business will improve the local economy and bring in higher revenue, while in the still longer run, it will throttle the city if they don't keep up with other cities which have a better cab-summoning system. Of course, that didn't bother the maritime unions when they drove away the ocean-shipping trade, and it doesn't seem to bother the unions which control the Convention Center, or the stagehands who make it expensive to put on shows, operas and concerts. Or, for that matter, the residents of the city who regularly vote a change of political control, every seventy years.

The Uber drivers explain that they own their cabs, and must keep them fresh and clean according to Uber standards. Each cab has a portable internet connection, with an Uber software package for which the drivers probably pay a fee, but the "app" is free to the customers. When you tell the program where you are and where you want to go, the central office uses GTF to locate and assign your trip to the nearest Uber driver cruising in your neighborhood, whose location is also tracked by GTF. The result is a binging sound in the cab, and a picture of the cab on a map in the customer's "app", together with a button to push to connect the customer's phone to the driver. So the driver, cruising nearby with another customer, can immediately shift to the cab-requester in about five minutes. You can tell him what color overcoat you are

Uber App

wearing, and how to negotiate the lane you live on, beware of the dog. In about five minutes you can watch on your portable computer-- while his cab negotiates the turns to pick you up, which he does, and zips you off to where you want to go. The company already has your credit card, so you just get off, and the driver zips away on another call that came in while you were travelling. The driver is often a lady, which fearful lady customers like to see; the lady driver is often a mother who likes to choose her own hours to work, while there is someone at home to watch the kids.

There are some features which might be called disadvantages. The driver is unable to call the dispatcher, so there is no way to notify the dispatcher there is construction at your pick-up point, or it's a blind alley to be avoided if you didn't know the landmarks, yourself. That means the driver doesn't wait very long if you are not where he thought you were, and although you can watch him drive away on the internet screen, he's off on another call while you stand in the rain. And the price of the ride is apparently a continuous auction, so you can watch it go from $13 to $5 and then back to $10; the truth is most people don't know what they were charged until they see the credit card invoice.

Uber Logo

The competition has apparently stimulated the local cab monopoly to produce an imitation app, called 215 Get a Cab, for the medallion folks. I haven't tried it yet, but it's heartening to see the effect of competition on an otherwise closed system with political overtones. The last cabby I engaged proudly showed me there were eight cabs within two blocks of where I stood shivering, vainly tooting on my taxi whistle. So, even the medallion taxis are better off for Uber with its destructive innovation. So far.

TOPIC 384 Right Angle Club 2017 => BLOG 1008 The Definition of a Real Philadelphian (1914)

The Definition of a Real Philadelphian (1914)

Elizabeth Robbins Pennell

Mrs. Pennell states the Philadelphia case with such guileless precision that it's hilarious. Quaker ladies can wield a rapier wit without hurting feelings.

There are several million people living in Philadelphia, but of course, not all of them are *real* Philadelphians. Elizabeth Robbins Pennell, a friend and biographer of James McNeill Whistler, tells us the definition of a *real* Philadelphian in 1914.

"I think I have a right to call myself a Philadelphian, though I am not sure if Philadelphia is of the same opinion. I was born in Philadelphia, as my father was before me, but my ancestors, having had the sense to emigrate to America in time to make me as American as an American can be, were then so inconsiderate as to waste a couple of centuries in Virginia and Maryland, and my Grandfather was the first of the family to settle in a town where it is important, if you belong at all, to have belonged from the beginning. However, [my husband's] ancestors, with greater wisdom, became at the earliest available moment not only Philadelphians, but Philadelphia Friends, and how much more that means Philadelphians know without my telling them. And so, as he does belong from the beginning, and as I would have belonged had I had my choice, for I would rather be a Philadelphian than any other sort of American, I do not see why I cannot call myself one despite the blunder of my forefathers in so long calling themselves something else."

—*Our Philadelphia*, 1914

TOPIC 384 Right Angle Club 2017 => BLOG 3718 Two Central Mistakes In The Design of Medicare.

Two Central Mistakes In The Design of Medicare

There are surely dozens of misjudgments in our health system, but concentrate on two of them. If corrected, they could transform the system, while if uncorrected, no scoring -- dynamic or otherwise -- will conceal our collective failure to address health costs seriously. Other problems can stand aside while these two are considered.

The first is pay-as-you-go. Its name is misleading, because the younger generation, mostly enjoying good health, pays for the previous generation's dauntingly high health costs toward the end of life. Medicare started in 1965, and grew for fifty years. The first generation thus was given a free ride, so my mother who died at the age of 103, represents a whole generation who paid essentially nothing for thirty years of expenses. This hot potato of debt was passed along for fifty years, getting bigger with time and baby booms. The burden of 18% of Gross Domestic Product became unsupportable, even with abnormally low interest rates. We must now liquidate the debt burden, invest the idle savings until needed for healthcare, and thus eliminate the annual 50% Medicare deficit to foreign nations. Quite a task.

An important result of replacing pay-go with pre-payment is the incentive to save, replacing the historical incentive to spend. Actual experience with HSAs demonstrates net savings in health cost to be at least 20%.

Using a Health Savings Account, young people of each generation **save for their own subsequent health costs, instead of spending immediately for anonymous demographic groups of strangers.** At this point, another unexpected bonus appeared:

Some young people have the good luck not to get sick very much, thus accumulating tax-exempt money in the account when they turn 66. In fact, most people do escape serious illness until about age 55. Since everyone gets Medicare eventually, current law turns HSA accumulations into a tax-exempt retirement fund, a provision which went largely unnoticed. (It's mandatory, while I would prefer an option.)

At this point, a second blunder by the designers of Medicare reached the surface. Medicare provided better medical care, made longevity increase, but laid bare it had added thirty years to be financed as retirement cost. Sickness cost is episodic, but retirement costs are continuous. Consequently, these additional retirement costs may eventually become several times as costly as the sickness costs they replaced.

I cannot claim it will be easy to scrape together a package of proposals to cover the transition to a considerably less costly funding system. But I have tried, and suggestions follow in this book. No health funding scheme other than Health Savings Accounts provides even a flimsy scaffold for addressing this new issue. Social Security does have such a mission, but it is hopelessly underfunded. I'm afraid we have to say this impending disaster is largely a consequence of Medicare's success. So this is the second of two big problems facing us: we failed to anticipate success.

But there is a third big elephant in this room which might be wiped out with a paragraph of legislation. Scratch any regulation and you usually find a lobbyist underneath it. Somewhat over half of the population enjoys a tax deduction which is denied to the other half, and that other population is restless about it. Unless big corporations soon yield to the demand for equality of treatment, there will be continuing agitation. No doubt it is contemplated to address this issue in the looming tax reform, and perhaps the defenders of this inexcusable situation plan to reserve their concessions for later trade-offs. But after seventy years of this inequity, one half of the public owes such a large debt to that other half, little *quid pro quo* is justified. Permitting HSA to pay the premiums for its required high-deductible insurance could accomplish this in a handful of sentences, eliminating the grievance.

And what might be called the fourth big issue actually offers hope, instead of despair. Medicare coverage for young unemployable persons ("disabled") was effectively broadened to over 90% in 1984. Narrowly higher costs were thus added to basic Medicare costs for 9 million of the 46 million regular Medicare recipients, rather than remaining lumped with the 30 million uninsured unemployables (requiring specialized programs.) These higher costs of average Medicare per employable person, have been overlooked by most commentators, making ordinary Medicare seem costlier than it really is. It's bad, all right, but not quite as bad as it seems. Documenting that fact, as well as shifting the medical income tax inequity to the tax bill, thus leaves only **two new issues to address: pay-as-you-go, and retirement funding.** That›s quite enough for the first round.

De-Globalization: Is It Real?
Compared With War, Is It Cheap?

GIC Logo

The GIC (Global Interdependence Center) recently held its 35th annual Monetary and Trade Conference, at the Gerri LeBow Hall of Drexel University. Its topic was globalization, and as usual the conference was outstanding. The conclusion of six prominent economists was that globalization may or may not be a good thing, but the unanimous feeling was announced that economists think it it declining.

That about ended the unanimity, because opinion is quite divided about whether this is a permanent thing or a temporary one, whether globalization will soon return or go away, and what caused it. This disappointing confusion seems to be the result of specialization, because the economists were also quite reluctant to discuss those aspects. War is the business of Generals and Admirals, annexation belongs to the State Department, and hegemony is the province of politicians. Quite possibly it reflects the Washington reaction to the unexpected election of President Trump, who declared himself an Economic nationalist after a decade of presidential encouragement of international trade.

Maynard Keynes

For one thing, the most influential economics book since World War I was Maynard Keynes' "The Economic Consequences of the Peace", which beside permanently besmirching the Treaty of Versailles, is said to have created the "science" of Macroeconomics. To contend that Versailles had nothing to do with the post-war famines and the crash of 1929, would be quite a reversal of attitudes within the economic profession. One would certainly hope we do not return to the attitude of Franklin Roosevelt, who is reported to have said, "I don't understand a word the man is saying, but we must do *Something*.

For example, I do not expect any respectable man to proclaim that war is a better way to globalize trade than negotiation is, but at least we can quantify the matter in economic terms by defining how much more it costs to go to war than to negotiate trade terms, or even how much it has cost annexing nations to do it their way, as distinguished between other ways. And since trade negotiations will continue before, during and after a war, perhaps it would be possible to judge whether going to war is least costly at certain stages of the economy, and whether it is better

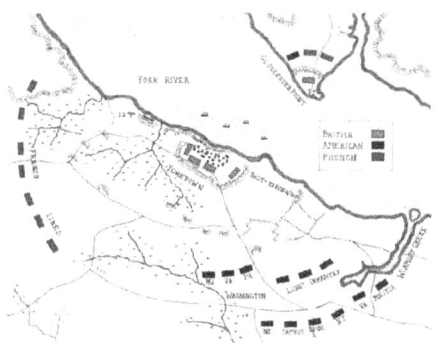

Battle of Yorktown

to win than to lose a war. The answers may seem self-evident, but even then it might affect behavior to estimate the quantity of the effect needed. This is particularly true about such issues as the one Keynes was describing, the cost of the loss of the British Empire. Here and there, the effects measured might differ from the conventionally expected ones. And the passage of time may change the opinion. For example, the French fleet hurried up the battle of Yorktown, because it was judged the Caribbean Island of Jamaica was economically more important than the measly thirteen colonies. How long does one suppose that attitude remained justified? Turning in another direction, what were the relative consequences of the Second World War, and the European Union? Or, the Persian Gulf War and the Invasion of Iraq? We seem to need a new book by Keynes or his like, about the *Economic Consequences of All Wars*. It doesn't seem to be economics which is expensive, it is lack of strength. As George Washington said, "If you are strong, people will leave you alone."

TOPIC 384 Right Angle Club 2017 => BLOG 3737 Award Seminar # 3940: Douglas C. Wallace, PhD

Award Seminar # 3940: Douglas C. Wallace, PhD

Although others spoke, the Awardee chose four scientists in his field to present the cutting edge of it. And at far greater length than there is room to summarize here. The first was **Aiwu Cheng (Shey-Shing Sheu)**, originally from Taiwan, but now **Professor of Cardiovascular Research at Sidney Kimmel Medical college, Thomas Jefferson University**. Dr. Cheng defined the role of the mitochondria to facilitate the conversion of ATP to ADP, essentially burning hydrogen by combining it with oxygen in the cell. In the case of cardiac muscle, ATP is exhausted in less than two minutes, and the cell will die. The cell responds by isolating the dead cell, and if enough of them die, the whole organism will die. The outcome is seen as the disease of sudden death in a person with an apparently healthy heart, but it

Dr. Aiwu Cheng

probably plays a role in heart failure, and death in general. In the intestinal tract, the bowel stops working, resulting in distension and fluid levels. When the person loses weight and then partially regains it, superoxide is released, probably causing distant damage to other cells by causing apoptosis. Dr. Cheng very kindly substituted for Sir John Walker, who was unable to fly to America on doctor's orders.

The second speaker was **Nick Lane, Ph.D., Professor of Evolutionary Biochemistry, University College London**, notable for theoretical books he has written about mitochondria, particularly emphasizing their probable role in sexual reproduction. Although a few ocean species differ, it is usual in our form of life to

Nick Lane, Ph.D.,

have a single set of nuclear DNA, and many sets of genes for mitochondrial DNA. The explanation seems to be the sperm cell contains no mitochondria, so mitochondria and the diseases they transmit are only carried by the mothers. Although some rare animals do things differently, mitochondria are exclusively transmitted by the females and their action on organ differentiation is controlled by the organ ratio of mitochondrial DNA to nuclear DNA. Essentially, that takes care of life, death, and sex.

The third speaker was also a Knight from England, **Sir Douglass M. Turnbull, Professor and Director of the Wellcome Trust Center for Mitochondrial Research, Newcastle, UK** . A practicing pediatrician, he is credited with discovering a mutation of mitochondria, the diseases it causes, and the legality of the 3-parent cure of the disease. The cure involves removing the ovum from the mother, sucking out the nuclei with a pipette, and inserting the mitochondria from another mother, with fertilization by the father's sperm along the way. The result is a baby with two mothers and a father. Apparently, such operations require approval of Parliament under the British medical system, and it took seven years of hard work to persuade all the committees to approve. This talk was given the day after the Trump bill discarded most

Sir Douglass M. Turnbull

of Obamacare, and loyal Englishman that he is, Sir John gratuitously commented that it illustrated the superiority of the British system. It was a little hard to follow his reasoning, however brilliant his research. He did comment that one baby in six carries mitochondrial mutations, so his own work will undoubtedly become famous.

And the final scientific speaker was Doug Wallace, himself. **Douglas C. Wallace, Ph.D., Professor and Director of the Center for Mitochondrial and Epigenomic Medicine at Children's Hospital of Philadelphia.** Doug fired scientific discoveries at his audience like a fire-hose, including the female exclusiveness of mitochondrial transmission, the utility of following tribal migrations around the world by sampling mitochondrial mutations, and the discovery that mitochondria were probably once bacteria which somehow got lodged within yeast cells. The significance of this point is that yeast cells are unable to burn oxygen (make ATP) and acquired what was originally the exclusive ability of plants. In any event, there are more mutations within the 37 mitochondrial genes than in the thousands of nuclear ones, and hence a much greater chance of finding cancers (or the cure for cancers) in one place than another. The practical difference between curing one common expensive disease, versus many rare ones, must be obvious. Children's Hospital must be proud of this humble man.

Douglas C. Wallace, Ph.D.

College for Prison Inmates

Marjorie G. Jones

The Right Angle Club was honored to have the wife of one of its members, Marjorie G. Jones wife of Jonathan Jones, as its speaker at a recent Friday lunch meeting. Both are Quakers, as you might expect from couples with those names. Marjorie told us of her interesting experiences with a typical Quaker concern, supplying college education to incarcerated prisoners.

In this case, she was not acting as a J.D., which she also is, but rather as a teacher, teaching college-level History at Graterford Prison to sure-enough felons, under the auspices of Villanova University, and before that, at Sing-Sing Prison. Pennsylvania comes out looking rather shabby by comparison with New York in these matters, an example of which is the Pennsylvania Law that no one may teach Social Science except with a PhD degree, even though they have a J.D. as she does. Similarly, there are four thousand prisoners in Graterford, while the much more famous Sing-Sing has only seventeen hundred. Pennsylvania hates to blow its own horn, even when the subject is fairly non-glamorous. It even goes as far as spell-check, which never heard of Graterford, but has no trouble recognizing Sing-Sing, up alongside the Hudson River, in Ossining, NY -- which is only half as large.

Graterford Prison

The Quakers of Pennsylvania conceived of Eastern Penitentiary, whose central theme was solitary confinement, hoping in the Quaker tradition for the calming effect of silence to soothe the prisoner into remorseful rehabilitation. Most Quakers would not see quiet reflection as a punishment, but the rest of the world under the leadership of Charles Dickens no less, saw it as hideous torment, cruel and unusual punishment. Most Quakers will tell you they rather enjoy an hour of silence.

Ever since their own imprisonment in the 17th Century, the Quakers have had a particular interest in helping the plight of the incarcerated. The rest of the world may yet turn away from prison as a punishment, because prisons are so expensive, costing more than it costs to go to Harvard, and having an incidence of recidivism close

Eastern Penitentiary

to 65%, plus nearly universal drug use. The Quakers, seeing That of God in every man, specialize in giving college degrees to inmates, and have a recidivism rate around 1%. Mrs. Jones frankly admits there are some people in stir who deserve to be there, and would be a hazard to society if released. Pennsylvania has little sympathy with "visitation" rights, which are greatly enjoyed by New York prisoners, while Pennsylvania is more attracted to privately operated prisons, with their incentive for welcoming more prisoners the better.

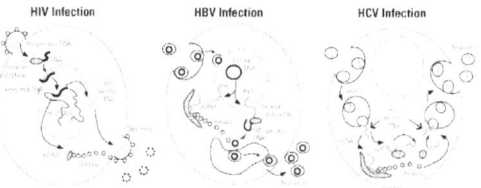

HIV (AIDS) and Hepatitis B, Hep C

A week ago, a new development clouded the issue of what should be done about the punishment of crime. For twenty years, we have had a cheap simple test to demonstrate the existence of Hepatitis C, but no acceptable treatment. Like HIV (AIDS) and Hepatitis B, Hep C seems to have got its start in homosexual males, and gradually spread into the rest of the community by "dirty needles" in the intravenous drug world. The first two are coming under control with new drugs and vaccines, but Hep C just festers on, and eventually kills the victim with cirrhosis. But last week, the whole matter changed with the announcement of twenty new drugs with more than 95% cure rate in three months, and unfortunately a $65,000 price tag per patient. That's about $150 billion for the known cases clustered around penniless American prisoners, to say nothing of what might immigrate from abroad. There are about 30 million American residents intentionally excluded from those federal programs Congress is now wrangling about, including several million incarcerated prisoners. If even the Obama administration didn't know what to do with prisoners' health costs, it isn't easy to see a federal solution to it, and since the states are overwhelmed by health costs already, they won't likely be eager to add to them, either.

Because we had a test for Hepatitis C for twenty years before we had an effective treatment for it, patient identity is pretty well classified. It will become glaringly evident that the people who don't have the disease will be forced to pay for those who do, and those who do will already have all of the common characteristics for being discriminated against -- black, male, convicted homosexual criminals, to which must now be added the accusation of spreading disease. The prisoners are mostly destitute, and Hepatitis C is contagious to the rest of the population.

On the other hand, it is simply unthinkable to turn these patients loose untreated, no matter what other foreign nations may be bold enough to try. The "solution" is apt to revolve around forcing the drug companies to lower prices as a punishment for curing a disease, and the rest of the population to suffer more taxes. Unfortunately, this is apt to concentrate public ire on criminal violators, homosexuals, drug addicts, immigrants and black people. It is also apt to stimulate a desire to eliminate prisons by constraining their budgets even further below humane standards. You can expect Congressional hearings about the failure of competition to lower prices, and indeed it really is unlikely that twenty drugs would spontaneously make an appearance overnight, achieving a 95% cure rate, all at the same time. More likely, the manufacturers hoped to recover their investments, before the disease disappeared. But somebody is likely to get flogged, perhaps ejecting prisoners from jail back toward the whipping post, perhaps by looking for deeper pockets within the pharmaceutical industry.

Awbury

Philadelphia has many arboretums, because the early Quaker families had abundant land and their religion prevented them from spending money on portraits, theaters, and other forms of merriment. Awbury is an arboretum in Germantown, started by Quakers, but it has evolved into something quite different from the others. For one thing, it is older, since Awbury in England is very close to Stonehenge where the Druids are said to have worshipped astronomical phenomena. There are no stones in the area, and it has been learned fairly recently that if you strike the stones, they will chime. Such chiming stones are usually found at point of furtherest advance of glaciers, so these appear to have been moved. The residents from that area migrated with the Quakers a long time ago, although the Druids dominated the region a thousand years earlier. It's in Willtshire, if you plan to take a trip there, although you will be disappointed to learn that the early settlers were of no particular importance in England, while the Cope family which started the migration were early migrants, but not so early as to earn the right to belong to the *Wellcome* Society with William Penn.

Awbury Arboretum

Arboretum

The Copes originally settled in Delaware County, and had what is known as the arboretum on fifty acres in Germantown as a summer place. The location is in East Germantown, just north of what is now Roosevelt Boulevard, and would have been a pricey suburb when the Wissahickon creek housed the first industrial development in the region. The Quaker families intermarried and many of them settled near each other and the extensive mansions of the estate, which was originally purchased from William Penn for five shillings in 1681, and the summer homes were bought in 1853. The source of the obvious wealth is not recorded by Mary C. Scattergood, although it is mentioned that many ships were eventually owned by the Cope family. One surmises that prominent Quakers met at the various Quaker Schools, primarily Germantown Friends School, although there was a scholastic network of Quaker schools and colleges, including the many schools on Schoolhouse Lane, and Swarthmore, Haverford and Bryn Mawr Colleges. Large families were the rule in those days. The settlers at Awbury were both numerous and distinguished, quite evidently close-knit.

The main history of Awbury was written by Mary C. Scattergood (*A History of Awbury*), placing great emphasis on females and tending to skip over the male residents and their occupations. Women had children or became school teachers, and while the families obviously prospered, the main family occupations mostly must be discovered from other sources. Copes of various ancestry predominate, although the line began with the first immigrant Oliver Cope, who was a tailor. Mary Drinker Cope, and Ruth Anna Cope were early additions to the family, and Mary Drinker married John Haines to start a long line of Haines members. Apparently, Thomas was the originator of the many plantings, which eventually stretched to Stenton Avenue. It is mentioned that the Cope Packet Line (to China) of many ships dominated the Philadelphia harbor until steamships arrived in 1901. The Reading Railroad had a spur in the area, running from 9th and Green to Walnut Lane Station.

The various surnames to live in one house or another at Awbury (there are six of them) included Stokes, Emlen, Haines, Middleton, Evans, Dimick, Yarnell, Hazen, Stork, Lewis, Scattergood, Moore, Albertson, Foote, Kneedler, Aub, Hazard, McGill, Kimbers, Paramore.

(A History of Awbury)

TOPIC 384 Right Angle Club 2017 => BLOG 3715 Dracula

Dracula

The Right Angle Club was honored recently to be addressed by Michael Augustyn, who is a sort of amateur expert on Medieval history and warfare as a result of gathering background for his historical novel *Vlad Dracula: The Dragon Prince*. He didn't talk much about his novel (which is unusual for an author), but gave a sickening description of Medieval warfare, and a fascinating one.

It seems that Ghengis Kahn invented or exploited the invention of the stirrup, which allowed hordes of horseback Mongols to defeat the armored knights of the Western world. But before that, the Turks invading westward had discovered that if you unhorsed the knight into the mud, you could then make short work of him. In those days, the Byzantine Christians were bitter enemies of the Roman Catholics for one reason or another, but the invading Turks didn't make much distinction, and beheaded Christians indiscriminately. Among other charming customs, they catapulted the heads over the walls into the midst of the Christian defenders of castles and walled cities, to soften them up, so to speak.

Today, we regard the death penalty as the most extreme punishment, and some groups are even agitating to eliminate it entirely. But for the Turks, the death penalty was only third in rank, preferable to being blinded in one of three painful ways, or to being impaled on a crooked stick. It wasn›t described in great detail, but presumably the crooked stick thrust up the rectum would perforate the colon, and the resulting peritonitis would protract death for two or so weeks. Mr. Augustyn was definitely anti-Turk, but one presumes imitation is the soul of flattery, and plenty of Greeks impaled plenty of Turks, once they got the hang of it.

Dracula was a leader in Transylvania, now part of Romania, and is now generally treated as the Robin Hood of the region for his defeats of the invaders, not described in detail but probably pretty grisly. Evidently, his evil reputation originates in the hatred between Roman Catholics and Orthodox, which sort of persists to this day. Even in modern times, people will justify their hatreds by referring to atrocities between the Serbs and their neighbors in 1328. When President Clinton sent American troops into the Balkans, including the First City Troop of Philadelphia, there was abundant evidence of contemporary hatreds and atrocities attributed to 1328, which must have been pretty notable. It reminds me that sailing the Atlantic Ocean in a wooden ship to immigrate here has the virtue of obliterating such fables, and allowing even Balkan immigrants to forget them. The jet plane keeps these antagonisms fresher.

As I sat there listening to this, it occurs to me that I don't even know for sure what country my ancestors were in, in 1328, so I don't know which ethnic group I am supposed to hate, and if possible, disembowel. There do seem to be some advantages to forgetting about history, don't there?

TOPIC 384 Right Angle Club 2017 => BLOG 3693 Passive Investing With Total-Market Index Funds

Passive Investing With Total-Market Index Funds
New blog 2017-01-11 03:53:57 description

What we once called investing in the stock market, is now increasingly called "active investing" because of one man, John Bogle. Mr. Bogle, a main-line Philadelphian, invented index investing (now renamed "passive" investing) as a competitor to "stock-picking", now to be called "active" investing. It's made possible by high-speed computers. What hasn't been much commented upon, is that Fidelity, nominally a Boston firm which is second in size, is actually controlled through a Philadelphian named Solmssen, through a web of holding companies.

The original index investing used the Standard and Poor 500 list, providing high-quality diversification, adjusted for size. It was probably selected because it had a good record of smoothing out three common variables in a stock portfolio. Other lists had good records, too, but generally the stock-pickers for the list were famous and therefore well-paid, hired by successful companies which took another cut for selecting such good stock-pickers and advertising their success. This arrangement selected stocks which performed well, but it added cost. When computers made it possible to construct an index of the entire stock market of a nation, or even the whole world, it emerged that such inclusive lists performed as well or even better than active stock-picking, net of transaction costs. Because the index changed slowly, transaction costs were fewer, and consequently fixed taxes were lower, because less frequent. Indices were then tested for different nations, different industries, different sizes, or any other sort of difference. While many claims have been made for particular semi-active indices, they all increase internal trading volumes, so their costs also go up, although slowly. At the moment, it is generally felt that results are very similar; it is certainly true that trillions and trillions of dollars are shifting from active investing to passive index-investing. Nation-wide, or even world-wide, indices are thought to be essentially investments in the economies of the whole geographic area. The ultimate simplicity would be to buy the certificate, put it in a bank lock-box, and forget it for a lifetime. So far, this is essentially how things have worked out.

In spite of the stampede-like character of recent trading, there is still a majority of stock in individual accounts. Most of this stock has accumulated taxable gains which would diminish in net value if sold, and simple inertia is also not to be under-estimated. If all such stock were converted to passive accounts, no one can say if the net result would raise or lower the final value of index holdings. Nor can one be sure the unsold hold-outs would be largely limited to insiders who have personal agendas rather than economic ones, eventually leading to unfortunate gyrations of the aggregate price which would lessen ties to true value. Nor can anyone say whether the habit of buy-and-hold will become so ingrained that people will hold on when they should be selling. All that might be said is that, so far, none of this has made an appearance. And meanwhile the sands of time are running out, the train is leaving the station. At present, the most likely prediction is that overall volatility will be reduced, but true value can be assessed by the P/E ratio, the ratio of price to earnings. And a lot of brokers will have diminished income.

At the rate things are going, answers to this sort of question will seem stable in about five years. Beyond that time, waiting for more answers will probably mean waiting forever. So let's ask the simple question again. Why not use some sort of a total stock index as a replacement for gold in the return to a gold standard? Forget about going beyond national control toward individual citizen control, because that answer is already predictable: traders will like it, governments won't. But governments are sometimes nearly immortal, and people aren't.

TOPIC 384 Right Angle Club 2017 => BLOG 3685 The Future of Index-fund Investing, Itself

The Future of Index-fund Investing, Itself

Bank Collapse

An abundance of threatening international situations might unexpectedly lead to a banking collapse, but since every bull market "climbs a wall of worry", it isn't a threat unless it happens. The introduction of a new international currency is either never going to happen, or it is going to be needed without much warning. It's needed in the developing world, but there's a long way to go before it topples banking systems in the developed world. At the moment, nation-wide index funds might make a perfectly satisfactory currency substitute, like the Spanish pieces of eight. Index funds are tested and available in huge amounts, and trusted by everyone who talks about them. They are growing fast and may eventually dominate choices unless something even better comes along. If something better comes along, it is hard to see why we couldn't let the market replace them as fast as people want to buy them. In any event, we have tons of gold as an inert reserve. The question is, will they hang around in their present form long enough to be a useful tool? At the moment, bitcoins are the popular rage to make people rich, but most people feel a secret currency is a good way to make people poor.

Of course, no one can answer such a vague question about a vague future for a vague development. But index funds are essentially nothing but bundles of stock certificates which are easy to buy and sell, easy to lock in a vault, and easy to carry. They have real intrinsic value which can change with the economy and whose value can be checked in an instant. If something better comes along, it's hard to see why you couldn't buy it with index funds. It's hard to see why two or more currencies couldn't co-exist, particularly if the co-existence was temporary and brief. It's hard to see why it couldn't be limited to central banks, who support local secondary currencies with instantaneous

Stock Certificates

appraisals of the mark-up premium. On the other hand, it's hard to see why it couldn't be divided into subunits and carried around in everyone's pocket, if that's what is choosen to do. Since we got along with Spanish doubloons for centuries, it can be assumed it will serve the purpose. Since ownership is registered, it's even got one certain improvement: you can lose it or have it stolen, and still have a way of getting a replacement. In a sense, that was Robert Morris' contribution to currency theory: if a wooden boatload of gold sank, it was gone. But if a boatload of gold certificates sank, the underlying gold was still safe at home.

Charles de Gaulle

Resistance from those it would put out of work can safely be assumed. Just scratch any regulation, and you will find a lobbyist, usually very well funded. But the hard core opposition would be from those who see that the currency has real value if you own it legitimately. Its value as a currency is that it is a real value, a piece of the economy, which you can carry with you anywhere. It therefore upsets the principle of national boundaries established long ago by the Treaty of Westphalia. If you want to defend this fact, you will say you could buy the country that way, by imagining a horde of "tourists" who open their knapsacks and demand what they bought, which is your economy. Some elderly people may remember the French battleship which Charles de Gaulle sent to New York harbor to demand his gold. It wouldn't take very long for that to be disruptive, as the more recent Irish experiment with lowered tariffs also graphically demonstrated with migrant corporations. Eventually, even the United States had to make itself competitive with the 12.5% tariffs of the Irish Republic. You will find, even though it is denied, that nations with weak economies don't want to be rescued by richer countries, so they will cook their books. A portable ownership of the means of production is not merely portable socialism, it is portable ownership of a corporation which may be indefensible legally, therefore leads to war if you try to exercise the right. So unless a simple prevention can be devised, sovereignty is the one thing this money won't buy, even with Brexit. It might some day seem useful to prevent economic sovereignty as well, and for that we must look to what the European Union devises for its individual component nations, since they don't want to adopt the American one. With the exception of the Civil War, we managed to buy our way out of trouble by having rich states support poor ones, since we are all Americans, right? Until we reach the point of industrial states getting along with slave states, it would be better to have national currencies, based on national economies, type unspecified.

Treaty of Westphalia

Until someone figures out a solution to that issue, a confederation of national currencies based on index funds is about the best we can offer as a short-term solution. You can gamble on long-term stability, but it's your risk to do so, just as it is today. Short-term is worth something substantial, however. Reducing the cost of trade would almost surely inject several percent of GDP into everybody's economy, net of the cost of doing it. It should be the basis of a bull market, for quite a while.

TOPIC 384 Right Angle Club 2017 => BLOG 3694 Equities, Not Debt

Equities, Not Debt

Great Depression

I confess to this feeling in myself: stocks are riskier than bonds. So I don't blame a lot of other people for having the notion left over from the Great Depression of the 1930's that stocks can suddenly drop, whereas bonds are rock-solid investments. That is an obsolete viewpoint which I know is obsolete, but I still have it. Governments have learned that issuing more bonds dilutes the ownership shares, effectively making the sovereignty risk the same, for both. But what makes this work is to go steadily deeper into debt. We established the rate at 2% a year, but wars and other catastrophes make it more than that. When we

Robert Morris

reach our limit, leadership changes, but we don't stop adding debt. We don't like to see that, so we skirt around it. Something will turn up.

So let's look at the history. When Robert Morris was running America's affairs during the Revolutionary War, he formed the opinion that governments should borrow all their revenue, while businesses might sell ownership shares to raise money. Corporations were just getting started in this era, but Morris extended this idea to the modern era when he was a delegate to the Constitutional Convention in 1789. Apparently he did a lot of talking in private, but this concept is tightly identified with him, allowing it to appear to be almost his sole contribution to the subsequent capitalist republic. It was a two-step method for individual citizens to control the behavior of a strong central government. During the early decades of the Republic the banking system emerged, and it evolved that big corporations sold bonds in bulk to create indebtedness, while individuals and small businesses usually borrowed smaller amounts from banks. When the economy collapsed after 1929, the impression was reinforced that bonds were strong, stocks were unsafe, and bank deposits were especially unsafe. That's not necessarily the case.

The process of gradually going off the gold standard created a slow steady inflation of the currency, so a dollar in 1913 was worth a penny, a century later. Indeed, it now costs the U.S. Mint two cents to produce a penny. The slowness of this attrition allowed trade to function during the century, and stocks accordingly rose, but the fixed value of bonds made them relatively unsafe over longer periods of time. After a brief, disastrous, flirtation with negative interest rates, bond prices limited their declines to the "zero bound", and

U.S Mint

sensible people avoided bonds as an investment. Speculators might make big profits from minor fluctuations, since doubling fractions of one percent could be leveraged to big speculative profits, up and down. But these profits were of the "zero-sum" variety, meaning all profits were at the expense of your counterparty's loss. Stocks, on the other hand, could make profits on a "win-win" basis. True, they could also lose on a "lose-lose" basis if inflation got out of control, but at least there was some chance of financial survival. Generally speaking however, the position of stocks and bonds had been reversed, and bonds were riskier. Governments don't like to have that acknowledged, since the Morris system confined all of their revenue to bonds. No one would freely buy government bonds if everyone believed this analysis. Except weakened governments, ultimately limited by the "zero bound".

No strong case is improved by exaggeration. There is still plenty of risk in the stock market. The aggregate value of stocks can go up and down, as a reflection of the ups and downs of the whole economy. But it is true that corporations increasingly form the bulk of national economy, represented by their shares on the open market. Governments are usually restricted to borrowing for revenue and, reaching the limit of their borrowing power, they are impelled to expand the scope of government spending. A resort to socialist systems is usually a sign of desperation soon to be disappointed, although socialism might possibly work when you don't need it. When you hear socialism praised, it

Stock Market

is questionable if even reserves will save you, because socialism (government control of production) wastes reserves even faster.

References
Robert Morris: Financier of the American Revolution Amazon

TOPIC 384 Right Angle Club 2017 => BLOG 3729 Girard College as an Entertainment Site

Girard College as an Entertainment Site

Girard College

For many decades I have hungered to visit Girard College, sitting like the Parthenon on the Acropolis of Girard Avenue, even decorated with colored searchlights after dark. In its very earliest years, the estate of the richest man in America was entrusted to City Council, but the corruption and lack of progress toward stated goals, forced modification. Unseemly behavior by political leadership caused the Board of City Trusts to be created with this monumental sum of money devoted to the education of "poor, white, orphan boys". For many decades, to be a member of the Board was the highest honor in the business community, and several large business empires were added to the responsibilities. Girard had the foresight to state in his will that no Pennsylvania property was to be sold, and when the downtown area began to surround Reading Terminal the wisdom became apparent. His farm was made into rental rowhouses of

Girard College

great profitability in South Philadelphia, a hundred million dollars worth of coal was mined in Schuylkill County, and the first Industrial Revolution grew up in the hinterlands in response to the blockades of the War of 1812. Girard's estate was well managed, indeed, was a showpiece of Philadelphia business acumen. He died with the greatest fortune in America, but that was only the beginning of the industrial power of the leaders who really ran Philadelphia. The school for white orphan boys prospered, not merely because of the corpus of the estate. Time wore on, however, and corruption wormed its way into the Board of City

Trusts, the neighborhood around the school deteriorated, and Milton Hershey was able to compete for the dwindling supply of orphans with the benefit of Girard's mistakes and successes, in his own orphanage near Harrisburg. Finally, the great migration of black people from the South took over the electoral dominance of the city to the point of dominating the courts and politics, and black girls now outnumber white boys by a considerable number in the school. Some members of the Board have spent some time in prison, but most of scandal attached to running an orphanage has migrated to the Milton Hershey School.

It is my understanding that the wall surrounding the school was considered to be entirely too high, so they tell me half of the stonewall is buried beneath the ground, to conform to the donor's wishes about height, but also to remain a more reasonable height on the outside. Girard also provided that no ordained minister should set foot within the walls, a provision which greatly discomfited the religion department. An old gentleman named Mr. Witherbee was once my patient, and told me he refused his diploma at the Harvard Divinity School graduation ceremonies, and spent the rest of his life teaching Religion at Girard College after the School found he had perfect credentials for the job, but lacked the stain of ordination. The President of the Dallas Federal Reserve was once a student at Girard, as was the President of the Insurance Company of North America when it was the largest casualty company in the business. Daniel Webster was engaged to represent the College in Court while he was still in the Senate. I'm told that the boys were dressed by Brooks Brothers, and on and on. I'm also told the new managers of the Board of City Trusts ran down the endowment considerably.

Daniel Webster

Well, I finally got a chance to see the inside of Girard College, when the Shakspere Society held its annual dinner there, and it is indeed everything it was reputed to be. The Society was in black tie, having cocktails on the portico of what looked like an exact replica of the Parthenon, wafted by spring breezes and later bathed in spotlights, just like the real Parthenon in Athens. There were real guards at the gates. Dinner was superb, held in a main library, beneath a 48-step marble staircase to the second floor exhibition halls, overseen by a curator, and filled with Chinese porcelains, leather carriages, towering book cases, and the like. The place was immaculate, and the staircases so wide you could climb dizzying heights without getting dizzy if you stayed close to the wall. No white orphan boys in evidence, however. And for that matter, no black girls, either. Looking out at Girard Avenue, you can see a splendid avenue stretching to the casinos at the far end. And the trees were so tall, you couldn't see what was behind them.

Annual Report 2017

TOPIC 384 Right Angle Club 2017 => BLOG 2930 New Looks for College?

New Looks for College?

The New York *Times* ran an article by Kevin Carey on March 8, 2015, predicting such big changes ahead for colleges, bringing an end of college as we know it. A flurry of reader responses followed on March 15, making different predictions. Since almost none of them mentioned the changes I would predict, I now offer my opinion.

Colleges have responded to their current popularity, mostly by building student housing and entertainment upgrades, presumably to attract even more students. What I am seeing seems to be a way of taking advantage of current low interest rates with the type of construction which can hope for conventional mortgages or even sales protection, in the event of a future economic slump. In addition, they are admitting many more students from foreign countries, probably hoping not to lower their standards for domestic admissions. They probably hope to establish a following in the upper class of these countries, eventually enabling them to maintain expanded enrollments by lowering standards for a world-wide audience of students, rather than merely a domestic one. With luck, that might lead to an image of superiority for American colleges, even after the foreign nations eventually build up their standards. The example would be that of Ivy League colleges

Kevin Carey

sending future Texas millionaires back to Texas, which now maintains an aura of superiority for Ivy League colleges, well after the time when competing Texas colleges are themselves well-funded. The Ivy League may even be aware of the time when the Labor Party was in power in England, and for populist reasons deliberately underfunded Oxford and Cambridge. American students kept arriving anyway, seeking prestige rather than scholarship.

Television courses seem to be a different phenomenon. A good course is a hard course, so a superior television course will prove to be even harder. In fact, it might be said the main purpose of college is to teach students how to study; the graduates of first-rate private schools find college to be rather easy, providing them with extra time for extra-curricular activities which are not invariably trivial. I well remember William F. Buckley Jr, pouring out amazing amounts of written prose for the college newspaper and other outlets, in spite of carrying a rigorous academic workload. I feel sure he did not acquire that talent in college, but rather,

Cambridge University

45

came to Yale, already loaded for Bear. I am certain I do not know what future place tape-recorded classes will eventually assume, but I do feel such courses would be most useful for graduate students, who have already learned how to study in solitude.

To return to the excess of dormitories under construction, the approaching surplus of them might also lead to a better use, which is for faculty housing and usage. An eviction of students from dormitories would lead to urban universities beginning to resemble London's Inns of Court in physical appearance, with commuting day-students, mostly attending from nearby. The day is past, although the students do not believe it, that there is very much difference between living in Boston and living in California, and the much-touted virtue of seeing a new environment will eventually lose its charm. It may all depend on how severely a decline in economics retards the traditional pressure to escape parental control, but at least it is possible to foresee at least one improvement which could result from fiscal stringency.

William F. Buckley Jr

TOPIC 384 Right Angle Club 2017 => BLOG 3471 "Sir"

"Sir"

In 1938 when I was 14 years old, I entered a new virtual country with its own virtual language. That is, I went to an eminent all-male boarding school during the deepest part of the worst depression the country ever had.

While it should be noted I had a scholarship, there is little doubt I was anxious to learn and emulate the customs of the world I had entered. My life-long characteristic of rebellion was born here, but at first it evoked a futile attempt to imitate. Not to challenge, but to adopt what I could afford to adopt. The afford part was a real one, because the advance instructions for new boys announced a jacket and tie were required at all meals and classes, and a dark blue suit with a white shirt for Sunday chapel. That's exactly what I arrived with, and let me tell you the green suit and brown tie were pretty well worn by the first Christmas, when I came home on the train for ten days vacation, and the opportunity to demand more clothes. As I remember, my disconcerted parents agreed to a new camel's hair jacket, for $10, which was also pretty worn-out by the following Easter vacation, permitting another campaign for proper clothes. Furthermore, the stigmatized "new boy" status was symbolized by requiring a black cap outdoors, and never, ever, walking on the grass. The penalty for not obeying the "rhinie" rules was to carry a brick around, and if discovered without a brick, to carry two bricks. But that's not what I am centered on, right now. The thing which really bothered me was unwritten, equally peer-pressured by my fellow students, the custom of addressing all my teachers as Sir. The other rules only applied until the first Christmas vacation, but the unwritten Sir rule proved to be life-long.

Boarding School

And it was complicated. It was Sir, as an introduction to a question, not SIR!, as a sign of disagreement. You were to use this as an introduction to a request for teaching, not as any sort of rebuke or resistance. Present-day students will be interested to know that every one of my teachers was a man; my recollection is, except for the Headmaster's secretary, the Nurse was the only female employee. The average class size was seven. Seven boys and a master. Each session of classes was preceded by an hour of homework, the assignment for which was posted outside a classroom containing a large oval maple table. Needless to say, the masters all wore a jacket and tie, mostly of the finest style and workmanship. They always knew your name, and always called on every student for answers, every day. Masters relaxed a little bit during the two daily hours of required exercise, when they took off their ties and became the coaches, but were just as formal the following day in class. I had been at the head of the class of what *Time Magazine* called the finest public high school in America, but I nearly flunked out of the first semester in this boarding school. It was much tougher at this private school than I felt any school had a right to be, but they really meant it. Over and over, the Headmaster in the pulpit intoned, "Of those to whom much is given, much is expected."

Sir

I had some new-boy fumbles. Arriving a day early, I found myself with only a giant and a dwarf for company at the dining table. I assumed the giant was a teacher, but he was a star on the varsity football team. And I assumed the dwarf was a student, but he was assistant house master. One was to become a buddy, the other a disciplinarian, but I had them reversed, calling the student "Sir", but the master by his first name. Bad mistake, which I have been reminded of, at numerous reunions since then.

When I later got to Yale, I began to see the rules behind the "Sir," rule. In the first place, all of the boarding school graduates used it, and none of the public school graduates, although many of the public school alumni began, falteringly, to imitate it. Without realizing it, a three-year habit had turned out to be a way of announcing a boarding school education. The effect on the professors was interesting; they rather liked it, so it was reinforced. The only time I can remember it's being scorned was eight years later, by a Viennese medical professor with a thick accent, and he was obviously puzzled by the significance. Hereditary aristocracy, perhaps. Indeed, I remember clearly the first time I was addressed as Sir. I was an unpaid hospital intern, but the medical students of one of the hospital's two medical schools, flattered me with the term. In retrospect, I can see it was a way of announcing that graduates of their medical school knew what it meant, whiles other medical school were just red-brick. Although they too had mostly graduated from red-brick colleges, their medical school aspired to be Ivy League.

Yale

If you travelled in Ivy League circles, the Sir convention was pretty universal until 1965, when going to school tieless reached almost all college faculties, thus extending permission to students to imitate them. Perhaps this had to do with co-education, since the sir tradition was never very strong in women's colleges, and denounced by the girls when the men's colleges went co-ed. Perhaps it had to do with the SAT test

Right Angle Club

replacing school background as the major selection factor for admission. Perhaps it was the influx of central European students, children of European graduates for whom an anti-aristocratic posture was traditional, and until they came to America, largely futile. Perhaps it was economic. The American balance of trade had been positive for many decades before 1965; afterwards, the balance of trade has been steadily negative.

In Shakespeare's day, "Sirrah" was a slur about persons of inferior status. In Boswell's eighteenth Century day, his *Life of Johnson* immortalized his characteristic put-down with a one-liner. It survives today as a virtually text-book description of how to dominate an argument at a board-room dispute. "Why, Sir," was and remains a signal that you, you ninny, are about to be defeated with a quip. It's a curious revival of a new way of immortalizing small-group domination, and a very effective one at that, which even the soft-spoken Quakers use effectively. Whatever, whatever.

The tradition of addressing your professor as "Sir," is gone, probably for good, except among those for whom it is a deeply ingrained habit. Along with the tradition of female high school teachers, followed by male college professors.

TOPIC 384 Right Angle Club 2017 => BLOG 3225 Pickett's Charge

Pickett's Charge

Pickett's charge is well-known as the high water mark of the Confederacy, the place that almost won the Civil War, but in fact was the place it was lost. Every Southern schoolboy can recite the details for hours. But the fact is, Pickett lost. Like the Charge of the Light Brigade, the losers are celebrated, but no one mentions who won the battle. Well, in fact it was won by three Philadelphia brigades, 13,000 in all, who were defending the bloody angle when Pickett hit them with 60,000 troops. Mostly Irish firemen volunteers, led by Philadelphia aristocrat officers, they suffered 50% deaths, but broke the charge.

If you want to baffle a Philadelphian, just stop him and ask who defeated Pickett's Charge at the battle of Gettysburg. Like the Charge of the Light Brigade, everybody knows who the losers were, but nobody seems to know who won the battle. After all, history is usually written by the victor.

Well, in fact, the battle was won by 13,000 Union troops stationed at the Bloody Angle, only two soldiers deep behind a stone wall, to defend against

General George Pickett

60,000 Confederate troops who had been concentrated by Pickett to converge on that point of defense. The whole Union army of about 60,000 men had been strung out along a farmland ridge, uncertain at what point Pickett would concentrate. At a little copse of trees at the angle of two stone walls, were three Philadelphia brigades, composed of Philadelphia blueblood officers and soldier volunteers drawn from Irish volunteer firemen, recruited by members of the Union League of Philadelphia. These Philadelphians, both officers and men, were to suffer 50% mortality in an hour of fighting. At one point they started to break and run when 150 confederate cannon were concentrated on their position, then rallied and held their ground when it was the Confederate turn to break and run for home.

General John Oliver Gibbon

Although General John Gibbon was the highest ranking Philadelphian in charge, and Brigadier General Alexander S. Webb was a New Yorker who had been in command of the three brigades for only one day, winning the Congressional Medal of Honor, the real hero was Lieutenant Frank Haskell.

Seeing the Union defenders starting to break, Haskell rode his white horse outside the wall ahead of his troops, and suddenly ordered them to turn and fire at the hesitating Union troops. The shock of this maneuver stopped the retreat, turned the troops to face Pickett's onrushing men, and routed the Southern advance after Confederate General Armistead vaulted the wall and started to attack the defenders in hand to hand combat. A member named Haskell was in the audience when Author Bruce Mowday told this story to the Right Angle Club, but Robert Haskell never uttered a word.

Bruce Mowday

Since this incident, I have repeated the story to dozens of Philadelphians, and not one was even faintly aware of it. It reminded me of Digby Baltzell's book *Boston Puritans and Philadelphia Quakers*, which expresses Baltzell's opinion that Quaker reticence is the source of Philadelphia's academic and political decline. My own opinion takes a different view of the distinctiveness of Philadelphia modesty, which was contrasted with New England by John Adams' remark that "In Boston, every goose is a swan."

When you run your eye down the list of Philadelphia Union officers who fought in this crucial battle, there is only one recognizably Quaker name from a city which even at the time of the Civil War was still Quaker-dominated. Quakers had been urged by the London Yearly Meeting to withdraw from the war tax issues of the French and Indian, and Revolutionary Wars, but a great many Quakers had fought against the British, anyway. By the time of the Civil War, however, the antiwar Quaker position had considerably strengthened. I can still remember Henry Cadbury reciting the position of his mother, a satire of the Battle Hymn of the Republic: "He died to make men holy, we will kill to make men free." The Civil War had greatly strengthened antiwar sympathies in the North, especially in Quaker Philadelphia.

Consequently, when the spoils of war were handed out, public opinion demanded that the heroes of Gettysburg be rewarded, without drawing any openly negative opinions about those who declined to serve. After all, the Quakers had initiated and led the battle to free the slaves, and shared a certain amount of wide-spread sympathy with the idea that the Southern

Revolutionary War

states were entitled to secede if they wanted to. And Quakers at the time retained considerable wealth and the power to defend themselves, if attacked, not to mention wide-spread ambivalence about the War. So, there was no great effort to persecute Quakers, but the idea of sharing the spoils of war with them, was just a little too much. Six hundred thousand soldiers had been killed in that war, and although Gettysburg contributed 51,000 of them, it was far from being the only bloody battle. It is my suspicion the constant decline of Quaker influence in Philadelphia since the Civil War, can largely be traced to unpleasant echoes of this more or less inevitable response to a postwar commonplace.

General JEB Stuart

It is unfair to bring up the subject of the battle at Gettysburg, without mentioning three other factors which historians cite as causes of the defeat of Generals Lee and Pickett. In the first place, the rather inferior Confederate artillery consistently overshot the target of the front line of Union troops, and fell harmlessly in their rear. Lots of noise, not much damage. It is also true Confederate General JEB Stuart was planned to attack the Union lines from the rear, but was delayed by attacks of troops under the command of, might you know it, General Custer. And finally, as Pickett himself remarked, "The Union Army probably had something to do with it."

References
Pickett's Charge: The Untold Story. Author: Bruce E. Mowday ISBN:978-1-56980-4 Amazon

TOPIC 384 Right Angle Club 2017 => BLOG 3736 Franklin Institute Awards Week

Franklin Institute Awards Week

Franklin Medal

The Franklin Institute began giving medals for scientific achievement in 1824. Since Franklin died April 17, 1790, it just goes to show it takes a while to recognize genius in your own midst, even when the genius would soon come to be known as the "most remarkable man who ever lived." Indeed, he would come to be known as the founder of the American diplomatic corps, and even suspected as the man who changed his mind about King George III, thus quite plausibly becoming the person who started the Revolutionary War, who devised the essence of the Constitution which has lasted longer than any other Constitution, revised the Postal Service as Postmaster, started one of the Ivy League Universities, wrote the best-selling autobiography, invented the Franklin stove, and became President of Pennsylvania. Starting nearly penniless, he eventually became one of the richest men in the country. Looked at from a distance, it also might be possible he was the greatest Rain-maker in our history, even though he spent 28 years in England and France.

But what he was without doubt or quibble, was a scientist. He essentially invented electricity, explained its nature, and started it on its way as central to the Industrial Revolution, by inventing the lightening rod. One of the commonest quotes about him is, if there had been such a thing as a Nobel Prize, he would have won it. But you seldom hear that particular quote around the Franklin Institute. Because the idea of awarding a prize for scientific achievement was not invented by Alfred Nobel at all, but rather by the Franklin Institute in 1824, almost a century earlier. It all started with the Bower Award, and continued for nine other prizes, generally referred to as Franklin Medals in nine separate scientific fields. Unlike the Nobel prize its scope does not extend beyond science, and even in the case of the Bower Award, it honors a business leader who exploited a scientific advance and made a business out of it.

Franklin Institute

The Nobel prize became the center of Scandanavian social life by utilizing the Kings of Norway and Sweden, justifying white tie and tails, and by giving a large financial reward, which has been greatly augmented by an investment advisor in Wilmington, Delaware. This year, the Franklin Institute decided to imitate that particular feature, awarding $10,000 apiece to the awardees, and hoping that generous American donors would get the point, that a little cash will quickly equalize a century's lead in astutely recognizing scientific talent. Most of the Nobel Prize winners had previously won Franklin Medals, so this year the trustees recognized the value of something tangible, to make a real race of it.

Nobel Prize

The Franklin Institute only holds eight hundred people, an audience limit which is exceeded before a single invitation is put in the mail, and the attendance price has risen, accordingly. That was almost solely due to the work and influence of Janice T. Gordon, who rose to be chairman of the event, but kept her attention focused on competitiveness with the Nobel, and award ceremonies in general. Consequently, the audience size level is limited by the seating capacity, a phenomenon first noticed with the Philadelphia Eagles Professional Football team. The football season tickets absorb the whole capacity of the site, so local people tend to get excluded. No one gets to see a football game except out-of-towners with season tickets. It will be interesting to see what Philadelphia does with this problem, but you can be sure something will be done. The Philadelphia Assembly solved this problem by sending tickets only to descendants of former attendees at the original Assembly Ball in the Eighteenth Century, but that limits the attendance

Janice T. Gordon

to Philadelphians--a problem in the opposite direction. Keep tuned. In other articles, we plan to describe presentations, so this audience will come to understand why this event is so popular. But the goal was set by the Kentucky Derby; the first horse to win the two-minute spring races sets the pace for others to match. Even if the Kentucky Derby horse breaks his ankle, his name is the one you remember.

The Franklin award winners have become more national and international with time. So, increasingly the awardee's travel has gradually increased, to the point where a dinner for the award seems inadequate for such trip to get it. So, the award ceremony now stretches to almost a week. On the first night, the awardee meets with his sponsors and fellow awardees. All day the second and third days is spent visiting high school students, for the purpose of increasing their appetite for science as a career. Selected for their promise, these students actually get time to visit with scientists at the peak of their careers, ask questions, and decide whether science is the

Franklin Awards

career for them; from all reports, this is a very successful experience. On the evening of the second day, a fancy dinner is provided at a neighboring hotel, and frivolity is expected. On the third night, a television announcer is recruited as master of ceremonies, the ladies wear their jewelry, and the gentlemen are in formal attire. The awardees and their sponsors are announced, one by one, get medals placed around their necks, and watch a professionally televised summary of their work, followed by a dinner for eight hundred dressed-up Philadelphians. And on the fourth day, an all-day symposium is held by colleagues selected by the awardee for an in-depth, state of the art, presentation of the awardee's significant area of work. There are nine such concurrent seminars, followed by a lunch. Whew! By the time it's over, the guests really know something in depth, explained by the most eminent scientist in the field. And, judging by the number of awardees who return to attend subsequent award ceremonies, they really have a good time.

TOPIC 384 Right Angle Club 2017 => BLOG 3735 Aaron Burr: Good Guy, or Skunk?

Aaron Burr: Good Guy, or Skunk?

Aaron Burr

Aaron Burr killed Alexander Hamilton in a duel, fair and square. Was that good, or bad?
Ross Kershey, a faculty member and coach at Immaculata University, recently visited the Right Angle Club and related the story of Aaron Burr, who prompted the Twelvth Amendment to the Constitution by being elected Vice President in a sort of backhanded way. He and Thomas Jefferson ran for President and Vice President in the Electoral College, but the ballots failed to distinguish between the two offices. So officially, he and Jefferson had an equal number of votes when the Constitution provided that the person with the most votes was President, and the second highest number of votes elected the Vice President. The Constitution failed to provide for a tie, and so Burr was within his rights to assert he was tied for the Presidency, since repeated voting failed to induce anyone to switch. Needless to say, there was a great deal of bitter comment about ungentlemanly behavior, and ultimately Jefferson was elected by a private deal, which provoked bitterness from the other voters. There were other grievances, and ultimately a duel resulted, with the well-known consequence of the death of Hamilton. A good many false claims were invented by various interested persons, not the least of whom was Gore Vidal, a Burr descendant writing "historical novels". As if the various true claims were not enough, there was a strong division between upper and lower classes on the question, with the Jefferson supporters sneering at the upper class supporters of Burr, who were disdainful of the low-life supporting Jefferson as not being worthy of the job of President. The background of the Sally Hennings affair may have influenced the electors, but were largely unknown by the voters, but which spilled over to the slavery issue in subsequent elections and formed an unspoken link to the emerging party system of voting.

Ross Kershey

Professor Kershey supplied the Right Angle meeting with a time-line summary of Burr's life, which is here repeated with his permission:

1. *Aaron Burr: 1756-1836, Newark N.J. - His father was president of Princeton University. One sister, Sally.*
2. *Both parents died when Aaron was 2. He and sister Sally lived with the Shippen family, in Philadelphia, briefly. Then with a 21 yr-old uncle.*
3. *Burr graduated from Princeton at age 16, as a theology major, justifying the description of bright Princeton students as "having the highest grades since Aaron Burr." He changed to law -- after graduation.*
4. *Revolutionary War--part of Benedict Arnold's ill-fated invasion of Canada. Joined Washington' staff in N.Y., (as did Alexander Hamilton).*
5. *During the N.Y. campaign, Burr saved a brigade from capture at the battle of Manhattan, including Captain Alex. Hamilton.*
6. *Burr spent the winter at Valley Forge (see Sonoma Tavern, below). Commanded a regiment at the battle of Monmouth. Heat Stroke--never fully recovered.*
7. *Resigned due to health. Continental Army's secret service (intelligence). Suspected Peggy Shippen Arnold (see #2.)*
8. *1782 - Married Theodosia Prevost- widow of a British officer and 10 years older. One daughter -also Theodosia.*
9. *Began the practice of law. Wife died of cancer- 1794.*

10. Daughter Theodosia, well educated - one son, who died at age 10.
11. Burr may have fathered 2 illegitimate children with servant.
12. Politics- N.Y. State Assembly, Attorney General of N.Y.,U.S. Senator, defeating Philip Schuyler, Hamilton's father-in-law.
13. Helped form Tammany Hall into a political power. Selected by Jefferson as Presidential running mate in 1800.
14. Disputed election of 1800 - tie: Jeff$ Burr - 36 ballots - influence of Hamilton decided the outcome. 12th Amendment.
15. Burr not really involved in administration. Presided over Senate very competently - in impeachment of Justice Chase.
16. Ran for governor of N.Y. - lost due to Hamilton's influence and smear campaign - "despicable".
17. Duel 7-11-1804 Weehawken, N.J. -Hamilton's son killed in a duel on the same spot in 1801. Both N.Y. and N.J. accused him of murder.
18. Hamilton's shot missed (on purpose?) Burr's shot pierced Hamilton's liver & spine. Died on 7-12-04, buried in Trinity Chuchyard in lower Manhattan.
19. Fled to S. Carolina & Georgia. Charges never pursued, eventually dropped. Burr completes term as V.P.
20. 1805-06 Burr conspiracy: invade Mexico? Establish gulf-coast empire on Spanish territory? Secession?
21. Plot included General James Wilkinson, Andrew Jackson, William Henry Harrison, Stephen Decator, Harmon Blennerhasset.
22. Plot never materialized - some troops, some equipment, some funds from Blennerhasset.
23. Gen. Wilkinson realized plot would fail, informed President Jefferson -- Burr arrested.
24. Tried for treason - Circuit Court in Richmond presided over by Chief Justice John Marshall, who was Jefferson's cousin and known to hate him. - 1807
25. Despite great pressure from Jefferson for a guilty verdict, Marshall interpreted the Constitution's definition of treason strictly. The crime of treason (the only crime defined by Constitution) as a conspiracy plus an overt act witnessed by two people.
26. No witnesses came forward, so no overt act witnessed by two people, so no treason. Not guilty.
27. 1808-12 Burr goes to Europe, looking for help from England or France. No chance. Napoleon.
28. Burr returns to U.S. penniless. Theodosia lost at sea, 1812 shipwreck or piracy?
29. Burr practices law in N.Y. 1833, at age 77, marries Eliza Jumel, wealthy widow.
30. Separate, after 4 mos, finally divorced.
31. Burr suffers debilitating stroke, dies in 1836. Buried at Princeton.

In the question period, two interesting facts were brought out. In the first place, there is a large rock projecting into the Schuylkill, causing a big bend in the river on one side, and a narrow defile behind it as an extension of Montgomery Avenue. Roads fanning out behind the gulch are now called Upper Gulph, Lower Gulph, Old Gulph, New Gulph, and several other variations on the name. At the entrance to the gulph on the South side, is now Sanoma Tavern. But in Revolutionary times it was Aaron Burr's house, with the assignment to guard the narrow entrance to Valley Forge. The department of highways once proposed to blast the rock away for commuters, but the Daughters of the Revolution wouldn't let them.

The second item of some interest is that Immaculata University, where Professor Kershey works, was the scene of the Revolutionary "Battle of the Clouds". Washington was retreating North from the Battle of

Brandywine, hotly pursued by the British, when a hurricane struck. Hurricaines were discovered by, who else, Benjamin Franklin, but not widely understood. All the troops knew was it was pouring rain, everybody's powder was soaking wet, and the battle was called off, forever to be known as the Battle of the Clouds.

TOPIC 384 Right Angle Club 2017 => BLOG 2379 Conowingo

Conowingo

After ancient disputes between William Penn and Lord Baltimore, the mouth of the Susquehanna into Chesapeake Bay is located in Maryland. However, the Philadelphia Electric Company got its power from the Conowingo Dam, and Philadelphia bird watchers by the hundreds go there to watch thousands of birds, attracted by millions of fish. But when the buzzers sound and the red lights flash, run for higher ground.

IT was once a major hazard of travel between Philadelphia and Virginia, to cross the Susquehanna River along the way. The river is wide at the top of Chesapeake Bay, and the cliffs are high on both sides. Consequently, the cute little towns of Port Deposit and Havre de Grace grew up as places to stay in inns overnight, perhaps to throw a line into the water and catch your breakfast. Today, these little towns can be seen to have millions of dollars worth of cabin cruisers and sailboats at anchor, at least during certain seasons of the year. In 1928 the Conowingo Dam was built about ten miles north of the mouth of the river in order to harness the water power, and the Philadelphia Electric Company put a power station there as part of the dam, to generate electricity for Philadelphia. It doesn't seem so long ago, but it gave a mighty boost to the electrification of Philadelphia and its industries at the end of its industrial decline from 1900 to 1929. Unfortunately, competitive forms of power generation have now reduced the dam's output of electric power to periodic bursts during the day, and Philadelphia no longer enjoys a reliable cheap water-powered electricity advantage. Coal and nuclear came along, and now shale gas looks like the coming future.

Conowingo Dam

Bald Eagle Fishing

Although water power could be claimed to be not merely cheap but environmentally friendly, the unvarnished fact is fish get caught in the turbines and rather chewed up by being sucked from the tranquil lake on the upside, emerging at the bottom as diced fresh fish salad. That attracts seagulls and other fish lovers to the base of the dam. Some fish escape the meat grinder and merely are stunned by the experience, floating downstream to be attractive to eagles, turkey vultures, hawks, and owls. The consequence is that many thousands of gulls sit on the downside of the dam, while hundreds of turkey vultures and eagles sit on the higher levels of the power generation apparatus. And hundreds of bird-watching nature lovers stand on the southern shore below the dam, poised with many thousands of dollars worth of camera equipment and binoculars. If you don't have a pair of binoculars, your visit there will certainly be substandard. Lots of fishermen are there, too, but depend on the waves of spawning fish at different seasons of the year; shad is particularly favored. You can now begin to see the prosperity of Port Deposit and Havre de Grace has a wider variety of attractiveness than merely sailboating and crabbing. There is, however, a large and ominous yellow warning sign.

The sign says you are standing on a riverbank where the water can suddenly rise without warning; if the red lights start blinking and the warning siren starts honking, immediately gather up your tripods and head for higher land. It looks pretty peaceful, however, and the people with tripods are mostly chatting happily with their friends. It can be pointed out, however, that about two hundred bald eagles are perched on the super structures round about. Cameras are mostly digital these days, attached to the rear of a telescopic lens three feet long, and when they shoot bursts of exposures they sound like a machine gun. So, the bird photographers follow a swooping eagle eagerly, shooting away and hoping to catch the bird in an attractive pose, throwing away the rest of the pictures. Good shots are called "keepers", which the photographer is happy to show onlookers on the rear view screen of the camera/machine gun. More sedate bird watchers carry binoculars made in Germany or Switzerland, which cost thousands of dollars and produce really spectacular images. It's unclear whether all this expenditure is worth it, but there is little doubt in the bird lovers' minds you are wasting significant parts of the trip without some kind of binocular.

Suddenly, ye gods, the lights start to flash and the siren starts to honk loudly. Not knowing exactly what to expect, first-time visitors head for the hills. The old-timers with a Gatling gun on a tripod are much more casual, picking up their apparatus and scuttling several feet up the river bank. The birds seem to know what the signals mean, scramble into the air, or start to arrive from far perches. The electric company seems to have received a notice that more electric power generation is needed, so the gates at the bottom of the dam are lifted and water gushes forth; the water does indeed rise rather rapidly. The birds divide themselves into two groups: the gulls circle in a thick spiral at the base of the dam, while the eagles and vultures circle independently in a second spiral, several hundred yards below the dam. One group looks for fish salad, and the other group prefers stunned whole fish. Photographers however much prefer the eagles downstream, circling and then swooping to the water's surface to grab a wiggling fish and running off with it. Some of the bigger bullies prefer to let others do the fishing, simply swooping to steal the fish. Ratta-tap-ratty tap go the digitals. After twenty minutes it is all over, and the birds seem to realize it before the water stops gushing into geysers. The river recedes, birds go back to their perches, and quiet again rules the land.

On the way home, you notice something you perhaps should have known. Interstate 95 takes people speeding down the turnpike, just out of sight of the dam. You get there quicker, but don't see the sights. Coming back from the bird watching parking area which the electric company provides, you are more or less compelled to recognize that U.S. highway Number One goes right across the top of the dam, up the hill and over the charming rolling countryside. Back to Philadelphia.

Emperor's Doctor

Kitamura

Almost trapped by the events at Pearl Harbor of which he had advance knowledge, this Pennsylvania Hospital intern rose to the top of Japanese medicine.

As told by one of his fellow interns who is now a very old man, Kitimura was one of the best interns the Pennsylvania Hospital ever had; diligent, dependable, intelligent and infinitely polite. He married one of the hospital's nurses, and they tended to keep to themselves, especially in 1941, as war clouds began to gather. About two months before Pearl Harbor, both of them mysteriously disappeared. Kitimura's wife later wrote one of her friends that they were in Japan. After the war, it was learned that she had been placed in a concentration camp as an enemy alien, and when released, had divorced him.

Still later, it was learned that Kitimura had a distinguished medical career in Japan. He kept up a minimal sort of correspondence with his old intern pals, inviting them to visit if they were ever in Japan.

In 1985 one of them did so, going to the largest hospital in Tokyo to inquire. Great silence ensued; unfortunately, the revered and distinguished physician had recently died. You knew, of course, that he was the Emperor's personal physician.

Rufus Jones, Quaker

Rufus Jones dominated the Quaker religion for a generation, bringing unity out of disunity, and creating some towering institutions in the process.

Rufus Jones (1863-1948) dominated the Quaker religion for two generations, causing a transformation which deserves to rank with that of George Fox, William Penn and Elias Hicks. A few elderly Quakers still remember him in person, mostly as an old gentleman who tended to lean backward while he spoke, usually hooking his thumbs in the sides of his vest. He was a prodigious writer, having once made a promise to himself that he would read a new book every week, and write a new book, every year. He kept that up for thirty years.

As a matter of fact, that understates his output. His published works were collected by Clarence Tobias at Haverford College, and run to 168 volumes, plus 8 boxes of pamphlets and articles. His family also donated his personal papers to the College, and they require 75 linear feet of shelf space.

His stated occupation would have been Professor at Haverford College, where his personal influence on the undergraduates was as profound as their influence was to be on the rest of the world. He is regarded as one of the founders of the American Friends Service Committee and the single greatest influence in re-uniting the two divisions of Quakerism, although some of the formalities were not completed until after his death.

Rufus Jones

One other index of his remarkable energy was that he crossed the oceans more than two hundred times during his lifetime.

Perhaps the arrival of mass communication has made it possible to have equal impact with less effort. But Rufus Jones stands for the principle in life, that it never hurts to work just a little harder. If high school students are thinking of applying for admission to Haverford, they better understand what is going to be expected of them.

Haverford College

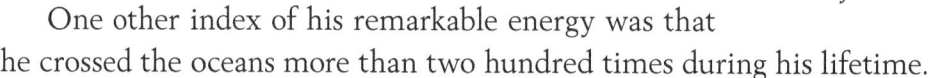

Bedroom City?

The Atheneum of Philadelphia

Inga Safron says her say about a city she grudgingly admires.

At the annual stockholders meeting of the Atheneum of Philadelphia, high society was out in force. Less expected was the featured speaker, Inga Safron, the architectural historian and commentator of the *Philadelphia Inquirer*, who gave a keynote address concerning the recent evolution of the city into a bedroom suburb. That is, she attributed this change to a movement among builders to transform large landmark buildings, like churches, into row houses in a a ratio of about eight townhouses to one church. That in turn was attributed to the ten-year tax abatement for new construction, which seem to her to be at the root of the recent transformation of Philadelphia from an industrial town into a place to live. That is, a reversal of the trend started in the 1920's, when the automobile caused a flight of the residents into the suburbs.

Before the meeting had begun, the new Treasurer of the Atheneum, Donald Roberts, had been privately giving his answer to my customary question, of whatever happened to Philadelphia -- by some accounts the richest city in the world in 1900 -- to decline and decay into the defeated old town of 1950. Don's answer was the city-county consolidation of 1856. This rather arresting explanation centered around the tax wall created at the city's new border, separating the much cheaper land in the surrounding counties by a wide strip of green farmland. To move further out, meant giving consideration to moving from the City entirely, initially provoking hostility from older businesses of Montgomery County.. But eventually it in turn caused family-owned businesses to cash out and sell corporate control to the stockholder controlled corporations peddled by Wall Street, which were essentially destroying the social fabric on which the city rested. A family owned business is local, and expects corporate control to pass to other locals who attend local social functions. Nowadays, however, if you are looking for a new CEO you don't pick the best dancer in the local Assembly Ball, you hire a head-hunter to look around for somebody in San Francisco. Such a person sees nothing unusual in borrowing from a San Francisco bank, which the locally born CEO might regard with horror, even if it might be a quarter of a point cheaper.

Thus, the city became oriented toward cheaper prices, instead of factoring in other considerations for decision. It's a plausible recounting, offering a different attitude toward changes in the social scene, and hence to modification of the tax code, or dynamic scoring of tax strategies, like enlarging the boundaries of the city at the expense of suburban competitors. It really sounds as if there might be two ways to look at things, especially historical matters. You hesitate to tear down a building where your grandfather started his company, for example, because someone whose ancestors came from the Balkans sees the same building as just an old eyesore in the road of progress.

Such considerations may not directly affect decisions like enacting a tax incentive to accept short term tax loss in order to create long-term tax ratables, but they certainly have an indirect affect. Who is going to benefit, and at whose expense? The builder who tears down the building will either go bankrupt, or retire to some other city; the person who treasures the past is likely to expect his grandchildren to benefit in the future. Such underlying attitudes are apt to surface in the form of a question: "Who will be living there, if the tax abatement has run out; and the stimulus to prosperity is forced to disappear?" To put it another way, who will willingly send his children to a lousy school?

TOPIC 384 Right Angle Club 2017 => BLOG 1219 Native Habitat

Native Habitat

Increased foreign trade, especially to Asia, has brought us some new plant types. Lacking natural enemies, they are taking over.

Teddy Roosevelt's friend Gifford Pinchot is credited with starting the nature preservation movement. He became a member of the Governor's cabinet in Pennsylvania, so Pennsylvania has long been a leader in the formation of volunteer organizations to help the cause. Sometimes the best approach is to protect the environment, letting natural forces encourage the growth of butterflies and bears in a situation favorable to them. Sometimes the approach preferred has been to pass laws protecting threatened species, like the eagle or the snail darter. Sometimes education is the tool; the more people hear of these things, the more they will be enticed to assist local efforts. The direction that Derek Stedman of Chadds Ford has taken is to help organize the Habitat Resource Network of Southeast Pennsylvania.

Gifford Pinchot

The thought process here is indirect and gentle, but sophisticated; one might call it typically Quaker. Volunteers are urged to create a little natural habitat in their own backyards, planting and protecting plant life of the sort found in America before the European migration. If you wait, some insects which particularly favor the antique plants in your garden will make a re-appearance, and in time higher orders like birds that particularly favor those insects, will appear. The process of watching this evolution in your own backyard can be very gratifying. To stimulate such habitats, a process of conferring Natural Habitat certification has been created. In our region, there are over three thousand certified habitats.

Of course, you have to know what you are doing. Provoking people to learn more about natual processes is the whole idea. For example, milkweed. That lowly weed is the source of the only food Monarch butterflies will eat, so if you want butterflies, you want milkweed. For some reason, perhaps this one, the Monarch is repugnant to birds, so Monarchs tend to flourish once you get them started. After which, of course, they have their strange annual migration to a particular mountain in Mexico. Perhaps milkweed has something to do with that.

Butterfly

If you plant trees and shrubs along the bank of a stream, the shade will cool the water. That attracts certain insects, which attract certain fish. If you want fish, plant trees. And then we veer off into defending against enemies. The banks of the Schuylkill from Grey's Ferry to the Airport are lined with oriental Empress trees, with quite pretty purple blossoms in the Spring. These trees seem to date from the early 19th Century trade in porcelain (dishes of "China") on sailing vessels. The dishes were packed in the discarded husks of the fruit of the Empress tree, and after unpacking, floated down the Schuylkill until some of them sprouted and took root. Empress trees are certainly an improvement over the auto junkyards hidden behind them. On the other hand, Kudzu is an oriental plant that somehow got transported here, and loved what it found in our swamplands. Everywhere you look, from Louisiana to Maine, the shoreline grasslands are a sea of towering Kudzu, green in the spring, yellow in the fall. It may have been an interesting visitor at one time, nowadays it's a noxious weed. So far at least, no animals have developed a taste for Kudzu, and no one has figured out a commercial use for it. When an invasive plant of this sort gets introduced, native habitat and its

Empress tree

Charles Darwin

dependent animal life quickly disappear. So, in this situation, nature preservation takes the form of destroying the invader.

But where is Charles Darwin in all this? The survival of the fittest would suggest that successful aggressors are generally fitter, so evolution favors the victor. Perhaps swamps are somehow better for being dominated by Kudzu, pollination might be enhanced by killer bees. At first it might seem so, but if the climate or the environment is destined to be in constantly cycling flux, diversity of species is the characteristic most highly desired. For decades, biologists have puzzled over the surprising speed of adaptation to environmental change. Mutations and minor changes in species seem to be occurring constantly, and most of them are unsuccessful changes. But when ocean currents change, or global warming occurs, or even man-made changes in the environment alter the rules, we hope somewhere a favorable modification of some species has already occurred standing ready to take advantage of the changed environment. Total eradication of species variants, even by other species which are temporarily better adapted, is undesirable. In this view, the preservation of previously successful but now struggling species is a highly worthy project. The meek, so to speak, will someday have their turn, will someday inherit the earth. For a while.

And finally, there are variants of the human species to consider. To be completely satisfying, a commitment to preserving "native" species in the face of aggressive new invaders must apply to our own species. Surely, a devotion to preserving little plants and insects against the relentless flux of the environment, does not support a doctrine of driving out Mexican and Chinese immigrants at the first sign of their appearance, like those aggressive Asian eels plaguing the St. Lawrence Seaway?. Here, the answer is yes, and no. For the most part, invasive species are aggressive mainly because they find themselves in an

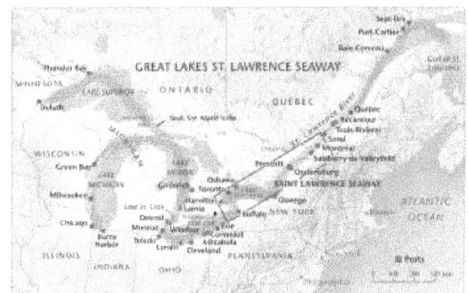
St. Lawrence Seaway map

environment which contains no natural enemies. If that is the case, fitting the newcomers into a peaceful equilibrium is a matter of restraining their initial invasion long enough for balance to be restored through the inevitable appearance of natural enemies. So, if we apply our little nature lessons to social and economic issues related to foreign immigration, the goal becomes one of restraining an initial influx to a number which can be comfortably integrated with native tribes and clans. In the meantime, we enjoy the hybrid vigor which flourishes from exposure to new ideas and customs.

In the medium time period, that is. For the long haul, if the immigrant tribes really do have -- not merely a numerical superiority -- a genetic superiority for this environment, perhaps we natives will just have to resign ourselves to retreating into caves.

What's Wrong With our Airport?

We've outgrown our airport, but other airports may be worse.
You can often judge the importance of a Right Angle Club lecture by the number of members who hang around afterwards to argue with the speaker, and if so, we just had a good one. The speaker was a lady, the new appointee as CEO, Rochelle L. Cameron . She's full of enthusiasm for her new job, but we have had a previous speaker in the same job, and could recognize the political problem immediately. She's white and her predecessor was black, just like the two mayors who appointed them. The political problem symbolised both the problem and the opportunity. The airport serves three states and nine counties. That gives it six U.S. Senators and ten congressmen, but it also gives it at least sixteen political bosses with a veto, maybe many more. China is widening the Panama canal for bigger container ships, but the Delaware must be deepened to compete with Wilmington, while the New Jersey Legislature has New York clamoring for a deeper harbor, and New York -- has more congressmen.

CEO, *Rochelle L. Cameron*

Airport

So that's one problem to juggle. The second is the airport is too small, sitting on 2400 acres when planes keep getting bigger and fuller. By comparison, the five biggest competitor cities are all approaching 10,000 acres, getting more crowded with people, bigger planes, longer flights, more hotels, more stores and traffic. One of the reasons Boeing's new Dreamliner is greeted so enthusiastically is that it uses shorter runways. And a little discovery appears: the new runway aims directly at a maritime crane, and can't be effectively used for take-offs. It would require millions of dollars to repair the problem, either by buying the crane or banking the runway.

And thirdly, our bitter legislative enemy, Pittsburgh, more or less controls the attention of the monopoly air line. Airline prices are mostly determined by competition, so we have high prices and a questionable ally. Over the years, Philadelphia has yielded a veto to the airlines and actually only employs a minority of the thousands of jobs the airport provides. The enormous parking is controlled by state-appointed authority, which in turn is controlled by Republicans who are unfriendly to the local Democratic machine, as just one example. The maritime unions have their own issues, and carry a history of destroying

Airlines Prices

Philadelphia's port interests, next door. Struggles over casino licenses lurk beneath a veneer of civility. Philadelphia has a unique combination of rail, highway, maritime, and airline interconnection, but all of those transportation modalities have competitive issues with the airport. The largest city in the state is treated like a wounded stag, with everybody competing to bring it down, tax it to death, or exhort a heavy price for cooperation. To some extent that's also true for New York and Chicago, but apparently they combat it better.

To some extent, the fourth handicap is our own creation. The lady who invented the hub and spokes creation is on the faculty of the Wharton School. The hub arrangement is good for the airline, at the expense of the airport. The airlines naturally schedule the landings close together, to please the transferring passengers, mostly going between short-hauls and long-hauls. That jams up the airports at some times of day, but it leaves the terminal deserted at other times, making retail store-owners unhappy. They dislike the airport location, and keep the rentals low. Some time ago, the airlines were given veto power, so they (or it) have the power to block a change from hub and spokes to something more locally favorable.

The Wharton School

And the fifth handicap is a lack of nearby vacant land, either to expand or to build a second airport. With handicaps like this, we wish the lady well. If she succeeds, she will be eligible to run for mayor or governor. As if we didn't have too much politics, already.

TOPIC 384 Right Angle Club 2017 => BLOG 3746 Let's Annex Canada

Let's Annex Canada

Are you as tired of global warming talk as I am? Here's a different plan. To read the newspapers, President Trump's revoking the Paris Climate Agreement is the biggest thing around. But it has no enforcement provisions, everything is voluntary, and its prospects of making the world colder are slim. The President is acting like a bull in the china shop, while the effectiveness of the document is questionable, indeed. The opposition party appears to have the motive of keeping him busy, so he won't have time to do anything substantial, and his motives are probably similar, except in reverse.

President Donald Trump

So I hereby propose a different global warming project, following the example of the cavemen. You will recall that during the last Ice Age, the cavemen didn't have a Treaty of Westphalia to worry about. So they adopted a different strategy: they migrated. Since 1648, we now have national boundaries to consider, so our way of creating room to move is to annex Canada. Those Americans who feel like getting colder would then merely have to go where it is cold. What would the Canadians think about that?

Paris Climate Agreement

Louis-Joseph de Montcalm

The French Canadians in Quebec might not like my proposal, since they have dark memories of Montcalm, or was his name Wolfe? But the oil-rich parts of Western Canada have oil which probably has some border tax they would like to be rid of. The Eastern part, the Maritime Provinces, petitioned America a few decades ago to annex them, so presumably they would like to have some gerrymandering, or possibly fishing subsidies would suffice. At least half of the Canadian political class would oppose, but they would be neutralized by the other half who would be in favor. It sounds politically feasible.

The attraction would be that it's cold up there, although Toronto and Montreal went underground to keep warm. The Arctic ice pack is melting, and climate change people keep telling us about it, with photos, and the Russians are selling tickets for tourists on ice breakers. If there are any Tories still around, they would vote Republican, whereas the people in Saskatchewan would probably still vote for socialized Medicine. The French? Well, they would probably have thirty parties and cancel each other. Certain parts of Canada are immersed in the Gulf Stream, and are warmer than Boston. I understand some provinces don't have taxes, certainly suggesting a paradise. From what I hear of the behavior of Esquimaux women, there are attractions for men, and the male surplus would certainly attract some American girls.

Arctic melt

So what are we waiting for? The Chinese or the Russians might get the same idea, and we could always sell it to them if we are disappointed.

TOPIC 384 Right Angle Club 2017 => BLOG 1493 Buying Corporate America with Cheap Money

Buying Corporate America with Cheap Money

Threat of recession induced America to reduce interest rates, and thus to cheapen the dollar. The rest of the world seizes the opportunity to buy huge American corporations on the cheap.

In the summer of 2008 Philadelphia was astonished to read that the rock of Gibralter, our family controlled Rohm and Haas had been sold to Dow Chemical company for $15.4 billion; corporate control will shift to Michigan. A week later, the Hercules Powder Company of Wilmington was sold, and then Budweiser Beer was sold for $56billion to a Belgian firm. The big old philanthropic families were cashing out.

While it may be true that taxes and philanthropic inclinations will lead this cash mountain to be transferred to non-profit foundations of benefit to the local communities, these sales are all a blow to the prestige and vitality of the cities which were once power centers of the world. Worse still, these prominent families with access to expert investment opinion may have reached the conclusion that it was better to have the cash than the business, or better to have the flexibility to shift the cash to more promising investment opportunities. Maybe they seek to diversify, or flee to gold, or invest in commodities, the next coming bubble. To what extent the falling value of the dollar motivated the purchase by foreigners or through foreign intermediaries is unclear, but it would surely be a consideration for foreigners to ponder. Worse still, these families may have decided they need to transfer more of their assets abroad. The glamorous investment advisors to large universities and major foundations are certainly advising their clients to invest much or even most of their funds to foreign investments.

The Rock of Gibralter

Under the circumstances, one would wish that foreign investors would shrug off considerations of national pride and concentrate purely on the economics of their transactions. But not likely; just as we grieve to lose these brand names, they must be thrilled to show off their new possessions, and eventually to use their control to shift power. The Secretary of the Treasury makes the unhelpful declaration that a strong dollar is important, since he does not need to continue that avoiding a steep recession is more important.

That's the way it is. Keynesian economics waters the currency, causes a fire sale of assets, and fires the flames of inflation. Now, what?

TOPIC 384 Right Angle Club 2017 => BLOG 3747 Is There Any Other Medical Revenue?

Is There Any Other Medical Revenue?

Taxation supports some elements of medical expense, so taxation has come to be regarded as a medical revenue source.

In our discussion of medical finances, we assume everybody's books will balance. What about people who don't do any bookkeeping, what about taxation? Well, the vendors of medical care keep books which include payments by individuals, and include expenses of running their businesses. Such items are either written off as trivial, or they are attributed to non-medical expenses, and of course there is the black market. But let's look at medical education.

Sweat Equity. In the old days, interne and resident salaries were zero, or close to it. Student nurses may even have paid some tuition to the hospital. No great effort was made to account for the value of such training, so its effect was largely ignored. Nowadays, however, the medical students often go deeply into debt, and pay back their debt out of salaries earned a few years later, paid for either by working spouses or government training grants to the hospital. Or, more likely, they are paid back out of salaries paid by the hospital but reimbursed by Medicare. The medical school indebtedness is often as much as

$150,000 per graduate, accounted for by government student loans, and the pay-back is arranged by the hospital paying salaries of at least $30,000 per year out of patient revenue, either government grants or health insurance, at least half of it government-supported insurance. It›s pretty hard to say which category of patient is paying for resident training, isn›t it? This is the back door by which government funding enters the scene.

Nurse training follows different but similar gyrations, making it overall pretty hard to assert these trainees are milking the system. They were once egregiously underpaid, and money fell in front of them, so they picked it up. It all comes to a lot of money, but as a rule they did nothing underhanded to get it. In fact, if you net out the loan repayment, they are still working awfully hard to make very little. The big winners are the hospitals and the health insurance companies, big losers are the taxpayers. Take a look at the administrative salaries, and you can see immediately where the money is going. The trainees can tell you they are righting a previous wrong, merely recovering their sweat equity. The administrators have a more difficult job justifying the institution's windfall.

We could go on, pointing to government self-protection leading to DRG, and consequently to moving inpatients to the outpatient area; and the shifting of nurse's training to the university campus where they seldom see a patient. But the thrust of this section is somewhat different. It is to explain how the 50% employer-based age group appears to support so much subsidy from so little surplus. Government financing is a large new source of support, making reliance on the patients for revenue considerably less necessary. It remains to be seen whether such relief is permanent, or merely a response to present economic recession. Since employer generosity too, is appreciably funded by taxpayers, rectification could lead to a downward spiral, leaving only the elimination of disease by research as painless relief. Even so, let me remind the reader of the expensive longevity- enhancement implied by that solution.

All in all, it looks like revenue enhancement is the best approach, and the Lifetime Health Savings Account seems the most feasible untried approach to it. Its maxims: the best way to have enough, is to have too much. And within the limits of reasonable compassion, make every ship sail on its own bottom.

TOPIC 384 Right Angle Club 2017 => BLOG 3668 The Plan

The Plan

It is time to present an outline of the proposal for replacing the Affordable Care Act with a cheaper payment design, owned by the subscriber himself. We first described its chief obstacle, paying for transition to it, not just because the proposal has to be shaped around that obstacles solution. It quickly becomes apparent people are so incredulous about overcoming a century-long year transition, they lose interest in details of it. Essentially, the solution consists of borrowing from trust funds after death, or possibly in anticipation of birth. This in turn generates income from extending the period of compound interest, which actually increases with a longer time period. Once it is accepted the protracted transition can be shortened into reasonable time periods, people are more willing to look at the overall proposal..

Most health insurance depends on overcharging healthy young people, using that accumulated surplus to pay for expensive old folks. Because people often change jobs, it becomes difficult for employer-based insurance to do that, so employer control of the system depends on the contortion of giving insurance as a gift to the employee. That allows the employer to set the terms, while increasing funds with a tax deduction. This questionable approach is only tolerated because it works, and nothing else seems to. However, in the long run it increases costs, and we are reaching the point where it has to end. With a plausible transition, we can at least look at alternatives.

The beginning of earnings happens to coincide with the least expensive period of life, around age 25. Children can get expensively sick, but someone has to give them the money for it. The period from childbirth to age 25 is a sort of no-man's land, neither self-supported nor assuredly funded by solvent parents. So let's assume children's health costs are donated by someone else, and the system really starts with approximately the 26th birthday. With the first paycheck, the new employee begins to contribute 3% of his earnings to Medicare. That's right now, and the employment period lasts approximately until the 65th birthday, followed by 20 years of Medicare premiums, until age 85, the present life expectancy. We suggest the payroll tax be paid into the individual's Health Savings Account instead of the Medicare "Trust Fund". If Congress would permit it, it would generate much more money if the premium expectancy were paid first, followed by forty years of the payroll deduction. That leaves 21 more years for a postmortem Trust Fund to make up any difference caused by starting later than at birth, reducing the implicit debt by 75%. Any surplus can be used for retirement purposes, any deficit remaining at age 104 can be written off. A table will show this system could supply ample funds for Medicare , and a variable amount for retirement. There are five special considerations, more or less optional in timing a phase-in:

1. Scientific Attrition of Healthcare Costs. We presently experience a period when new curative drugs costing pennies to manufacture, are being sold for eighty thousand dollars per treatment. Presumably this will be a brief period because no government can tolerate it for long. After turmoil is overcome, we can expect a series of scientific discoveries will eliminate many health costs, often preceded by a brief period of raising them, first. It may be tumultuous, but the eventual outcome will be substantial lowering of before-inflation costs of medical care. It might require a century, although probably will be considerably sooner, before we see health costs approaching those of the first-year and last-years of life. Executives of pharmaceutical companies may have other plans, but I have confidence in scientists› love of fame, driven by thirty or forty billions a year of research dollars, to sweep contrary trends aside. In the coming century, you can share my confidence that after-inflation health costs will come down. It will be up to Congress to be sure such savings are retained within the health system, and not spent on battleships, or new substitutes for sickness care.

2. Not a Single-Payer System, but Pearls on a String, Linked by Escrowing. This is essentially the same problem the Constitutional Congress faced in 1789. One side justifiably wanted a powerful central government for taxes and defense. In time, the central government was given a few enumerated powers by the Tenth Amendment to accomplish these goals, but everything else remained locally controlled. The dual problems were resolved with a dual ("federalized") system, which lasted 80 years until slavery and the Civil War broke it apart. Applying the same principles to Healthcare financing faces the same sort of issue, with the major difference that Healthcare financing is destined to get easier in spurts, constantly illustrating hope for the future. What holds it together is **escrow** a binding agreement to do what you promised unless some third party custodian decides you need an exception. The present four components are held together by escrow accounts, each ship on its own bottom, with a court system to allow for occasional special circumstances for one component to subsidize another. Other entities could add pearls to the necklace as desired. It has its fragilities, but it ought to last a century. If it doesn›t seem to be working, a single payer›s flaws can still be re-examined. But that›s why we must wait to see what Obamacare really costs, with subpoena power to be sure the data reflects the complexities. The working age population in ACA really ought to produce surplus revenue, but indications are it wants to be subsidized. For the present, approximately revenue-neutral would suffice.

3. Component-shifting, Replacing Hidden Cost-shifting. The lifetime cost curve of healthcare is J-shaped from birth to death. Both the balancing problem and the revenue solution revolve around keeping revenue and cost manageably in balance at each stage, so transfer systems are minimized, not exaggerated. As a generalization, our proposal depends on **moving payment compartments to other stages of the J-shaped curve**. Obsterical-pediatric costs are shifted from the mother to the child. The child's cost is shifted to investment-overfunded Medicare; male-female costs are equalized by removing them from the mother. The overall effect is to transfer obstetrical/childhood costs from single mothers and employers to Medicare (from the far end of the J-shaped curve to the opposite end), which is overfunded by the tail end of the compound interest curve. It's inevitably a little lumpy, and the final result must be smoothed out with the familiar tricks of accountants. It may seem difficult to persuade a dozen industry executives to shift business components like checkers, but it's a whole lot easier than persuading millions of customers to rearrange their health insurance habits. The new source of revenue is **investment income from the currently indolent revenue stream**, so there's considerable extra revenue to pacify a few losers.

The specifics are: transfer obstetrics/pediatrics from mother to child, donate that cost (supposedly $18,000) at birth to the Health Savings Account of the child, and eventually to his Medicare voluntary buy-out escrow at age 65. Any surplus is used for retirement, less buy-out costs for last-year of life re-insurance and childhood costs. (By the way, I bet we will find it doesn't cost $18,000 to bear and support a child; much of that big-ticket cost must be cost-shifted accounting maneuvers for malpractice, bad debts, etc.)

4. Computers: Finance Industry Suffers, Amateur Investors Prosper. Burton Malkiel showed a *Random Walk Down Wall Street* was mostly superior to the sharp-pencilled judgment of experts, while John Bogle made economy-wide investing a practicality, with index funds. Adjusted for fees, it was pretty hard for an investor to improve on low-cost total market index funds, just buy ‹em and forget ‹em.

Bogle's funds now total in the trillions of dollars, still growing fast, with only the crooked ones left to worry about, although the year you were born and the year you happen to die will affect the result beyond anyone's control. Otherwise, this approach will suddenly give millions of people superior results cheaply. When you compound the results for most of a century, a few tenths of a percent difference in return make a big difference in final outcome.

On the other hand, risky investments offer higher returns, so **total market index funds** must be chosen with care. The narrow index funds, by industry for example, are not what we are describing. Our present calculation is that a steady 6.7% average return will suffice for a medical lifetime. Professor Ibbotson of Yale reports the stock market has averaged 10-11% for the past century, and inflation has averaged 3%; the result is 8% real return to be split between Wall Street and the investor, When you consider who is taking what risk, the investor has a reasonable argument he deserves (but often does not get) 6.7%. And when you observe the violence with which lobbyists reject mandatory fiduciary (the customer›s interest ahead of the intermediary›s) relationships where 1% is at stake, it won›t be an easy settlement.

5. First Year and Last Year of Life Re-insurance. Two things make this transition idea possible. Not only is 50% of health cost concentrated in Medicare, but 50% of that is concentrated in the last four years of life. Secondly, the two halves of Medicare revenue stream can be separated by paying cost components into different escrow funds, re-united after death and/or borrowed, as seems expedient.

Effectively, this can remove half of Medicare cost from the main stream, and it's the half which will shrink from scientific advances of the future. The terminal care half is more resistant to shrinking, is payable after death, and therefore puts less pressure on transition, demanding expediency only for half the costs. Essentially, this dual approach is an alternative or supplement, to Postmortem Transition Trust Funds. If both methods are employed, the transition phase can be considerably shortened. If half of Medicare cost is already "in the bank", it should also reassure many older subscribers of its safety.

It's presently difficult to know what to do with First Year of Life Insurance until we are more certain of its real cost. It's held in reserve until we can judge what its urgency is.

TOPIC 384 Right Angle Club 2017 => BLOG 1639 Steep Yield-Curves Subsidize Banks

Steep Yield-Curves Subsidize Banks

The up-sloping federal interest rate curve is a subsidy to banks, just as surely as farm price supports are subsidies to farmers.

The steepness of the federal interest rate curve on a graph -- three-month treasury bills pay less interest than ten-year government debt, with yields for intervening time durations sloping from low to high -- is all a carefully maintained function of the Federal Reserve. The slope of this curve in the newspapers quickly summarizes current Fed policy. The Federal Reserve mainly controls the money supply by issuing or retiring short-term government debt; the effect upon supply by such action raises or lowers short-term rates, which in turn "changes the slope of the yield curve at the short end". The Fed 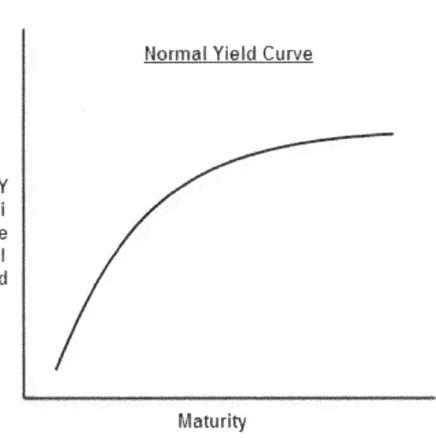 ordinarily ignores the cost of longer term debt, leaving that to be determined by the public bond markets. Less often, the Federal Reserve buys or sells long-term treasury bonds to modify long-term yields, or to adjust the international value of the dollar. By affecting rates at either end of the curve, change in the curve's slope is the result. Sometimes that's intended, and sometimes it just can't be avoided.

Because banks pay interest to depositors at around the short-term rate, while the same banks charge interest rates to borrowers at about the higher federal long-term rate, the current slope of the curve is said to be the main determinant of bank profits. In fact, banks charge whatever the market will bear, and their profitability mainly reflects the cost of the money, which the Fed has the power to set. Banks borrow short, and lend long. If the Federal Reserve artificially cheapens costs for the banks, then bank profits get fattened by public subsidy. Of course, it works the other way as well; in a banking crisis, the yield curve can be forcibly steepened to rescue banks from failure, temporarily sacrificing ideal monetary levels for the purpose. For the most part, what's good for banks is good for the economy; but it turns out bank profits are artificially subsidized much of the time. This artificially widened yield curve eventually punishes retirees and other savers by lowering interest rates on their savings accounts, or else it could punish debtors by increasing the interest rate they pay on mortgages and other credit. For political reasons, the pain is usually shared among voting blocs. It can be argued this subtle subsidy of banks by the public creates the compensating benefit of economic stability despite occasional bubbles and recessions like the present one. However, the Federal Reserve system has operated for almost a century, revealing an enduring bias in favor of inflation, i.e, the subsidy of debtors by creditors. Present policy intentionally allows a steady rate of 2-3% inflation, and the century-long effect of such policy since 1913 has been to increase the price of gold from $17 to $900 an ounce. A penny then is a dollar now, making no allowance for income tax shrinkage of such fictitious gains. Overall, the effect of semi-stabilizing the yield curve is to reward banks and debtors, extracting this subsidy from creditors and retirees. To go a step further, independent of the Federal Reserve but by government action, retirees have been compensated in the past by unearned Social Security payments. The payment imbalance of the entitlement programs is admittedly about to shift in the other direction in a few years. All this is rough math, with many individual exceptions; but the initial effect of the Federal Reserve system is to benefit bank profits at the expense of creditors. If we assume creditors react by demanding higher interest rates to compensate for the cost, bank stability is being maintained by increasing interest rates by 2-3%, mostly paid for by borrowers.

Is this standardless monetary standard worth its inflationary cost? Compared with a strict gold standard, yes, it probably is. A limited supply of gold to support a constantly growing economy once led to deflation and economic instability, and would do so again. An economy without a hard monetary standard responds to politics, is inevitably inflationary. The political independence of the Federal Reserve is dubious at best, and constantly under populist attack. So slow steady inflation seems to be one part of the system we can live with, in order to avoid either deep deflations or galloping inflations. Gradual low inflation may well be the best compromise we can devise, assuming the method of achieving it is otherwise tolerable. The 2008-2010 banking crisis, however, may be a moment of discovery that market systems must also be able to rely on the assumption that almost every bidder in an auction is limited by his pocket book. When two or more determined bidders are eager to buy but unlimited in resources, price ceases to have restraining power and becomes irrational. A marketplace can tolerate a few bidding frenzies, but excessively flexible monetary systems lead to bubbles in small markets, explosions in big ones. Disregard of price is particularly exaggerated by globalized trading systems, where customary prices are soon forgotten by abstraction within a virtual environment of essentially unlimited bidding power by essentially unlimited numbers of bidders. For bidding to stop, all bidders but one must run out of discretionary money.

The Marriage of Figaro, Huzzah!

A recent performance of *The Marriage of Figaro* reminds us that it had strong Philadelphia beginnings which recent immigrants from other cities don›t seem to know about.

The Marriage of Figaro

Whether it was a happenstance or the start of a trend, the recent performance of Mozart's *Marriage of Figaro* was among a handful of best operas I have ever seen. Or heard, if that is a better figure of speech. Perhaps management was only seizing an opportunity provided by the recent turmoils of the Philadelphia Orchestra; time will tell. The *Marriage of Figaro* may not be the best opera ever written, since it is the work of a young composer genius who failed to live long enough to mature into his final style (forshadowed by *The Requiem*), with a near-perfect rendition of a certain style of opera limited by traditions to the Eighteenth Century, and necessarily limited in the instruments available to a small Central European court comedy.

Philadelphia Opera

In some ways, it illustrates the fifteen or so early comedies of Shakespeare, all of which would have been improved by music and women players. Some are better renditions than others, but they all sort of seem alike. A Shakespearean comedy set to music, might be a way to describe it. Although it has star performers, in a certain sense it has ten central characters, five male and five female. All of these get their moment of solo prominence, while two of them (one male and one female) got the final bows to rising applause from a standing audience. Nevertheless, it is the performance of the entire company which delights the audience. It had one sour note at the beginning last night, and it was a little too long, but these seemed the rough edges of a nervous young performance, not the embarrassments of some overweight visiting stars.

Count Pierre Beaumarchais

This is after all Philadelphia, and one serious local flaw must be mentioned. The program mentioned Mozart, and the librettist Lorenzo da Ponte, but the historical roots of this opera apparently escaped the notice of management. The opera is a derivative of a play by Beaumarchais, who played a central role in the American Revolution. Count Pierre Beaumarchais was watch-maker to King Louis, as a result of inventing the escapement that made the pocket watch possible. As such, he was a member of the Court, but King Louis XVI didn't know what to do with a famous inventor who persisted in flitting about the Court delivering *billet doux* to amorous courtiers and ladies of the Court. So he was dispatched as a spy to the English Court, and became infatuated with the revolutionary ideas of John Wilkes. Returning to the French Court, Beaumarchais persuaded Louis that what the rebels needed was gunpowder. Eventually, this led to a French boat loaded with gunpowder arriving at a party given by Robert Morris, asking if it was possible to speak to George Washington.

Unfortunately Washington was at Trenton, trying to decide if he could risk an attack on Trenton, in spite of lack of gunpowder. So Morris arranged a meeting, the eventual outcome of which was winning at Trenton and Princeton, later Saratoga, and Benjamin Franklin exaggerating these victories into an alliance with France which won the Revolution. Franklin became great friends with Mozart, and sent him a rendition of the Armonica, a musical instrument Franklin invented which wowed 'em in Europe. Meanwhile, Beaumarchais wrote his play and Mozart converted it into an opera, useful as propaganda in the French Revolution.

Madam Butterfly

It is probably a reflection of the many recent immigrants to Philadelphia from other cities who now dominate our entertainment scene,, that this vital piece of history is not even mentioned in the program notes, much of which took place a few blocks from what is now the Academy of Music. By the way, much the same fate befell *Madam Butterfly*, written on a table of the Franklin Inn, only one block from the Academy.

TOPIC 384 Right Angle Club 2017 => BLOG 3723 Hepatitis C Has Been Cured: Tell All Your Friends.

Hepatitis C Has Been Cured: Tell All Your Friends.

During many medical meetings, I developed two generalizations: if one paper in three is excellent, or if the whole meeting produces one shocking discovery, you are having a good meeting. Two thirds of the time, if you let your mind wander, you haven't missed much. So imagine my surprise, when a 6-hour meeting recently related four formerly incurable diseases with new successful treatments, plus a new slant about how rare diseases spread, and a disturbing possible insight into the medical economics of pharmaceutical marketing.

Medical Meetings

Another insight about rare diseases was that certain diseases may be rarities in America, but are common in some foreign countries. Perhaps this disparity was due to differences in hygiene or nutrition, but no, DNA testing shows they are inherited. Genghis Kahn or somebody like him, seems to have spread a mutation around his neighborhood, and poor transportation kept these diseases local. But recent globalization increased foreign immigration, so these diseases are now commoner in America, when we thought they were local mutations. The new cures? They are for biliary cirrhosis, Hepatitis C, hemochromatosis, and Non-alcoholic fatty liver. Having said that, let's narrow our attention to the non-scientific one, the one about drug pricing.

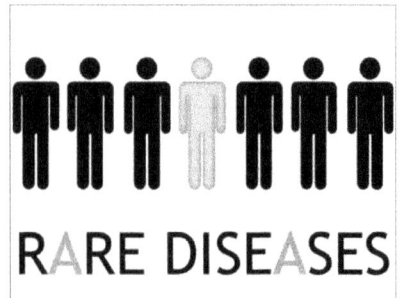
Rare Diseases

First, some background about Hepatitis C. Like HIV (AIDS) in its early stages, it was mostly confined to males, because it was initially spread by male to male sexual contact in prisons, along with intravenous drug abuse for the same reason. (Let me tell you, if you weren't a drug abuser when you went into prison, you will very likely be one when you get out.) The gay community rattled the cage for more research and the result has been a great decline in Hepatitis B and HIV-AIDS, but Hepatitis C proved much more stubborn. For twenty or so years, we had a test which detected the presence of Hep C, but we essentially had no cure,

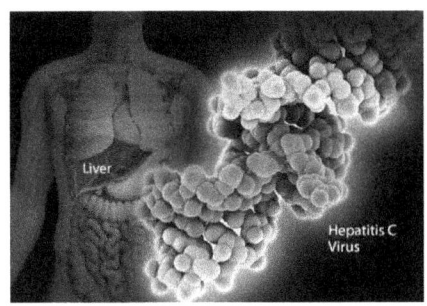
Hepatitis C

with the possible exception of Interferon, which made people deathly sick for a year and had only a 30% cure rate. Most patients refused to go alomg with this treatment, and for years I told most patients that in their position, I would take my chances on a better treatment coming along, rather than subject myself to this grief. Well, today I learned the tables had turned. About twenty drugs, in five classes, had more than a 95% chance of cure in three months, with comparatively little toxicity. All on a single projection slide. The speaker said they were contemplating a campaign to eradicate the disease entirely by 2020, while saying there would be a campaign to eradicate it by 2030, just to be conservative.

Well, I stopped off at one of the drug company booths to help myself to a free lollipop, and chatted with the drug representative. The drug was expensive, like $60,000 for a three month course of treatment, plus MRIs and other tests to monitor it, plus doctor and hospital charges. Let's guess it comes to $100,000 per patient. Wikepedia tells me there are millions and millions of patients with the disease, and the speaker guessed it was 1,600,000 in America. I suppose the drug company thinks no one can multiply, because that comes to about $160 billion dollars. Competition was supposed to lower the cost, but the initial reaction was

Drug Prices

a rush to recover research and development costs before the disease disappeared. Even that wasn't a satisfying answer, because neither prison inmates nor recent prison inmates could possibly afford it. Most of this projected cost would fall on state Medicaid. Whether there is any connection between this set of associations and the Tea Party rebellion against restraining Medicaid is conjectural. But it is certainly strange that a disease which took so long to find a cure, would suddenly find twenty cures at one meeting. The drug rep responded that if you just call the drug company -- don't call your hospital or health insurance company -- the drug company will almost always find a way around the problem without substantial cost. That's fine, but $160 billion? Nobody but the federal government has that kind of money, and it's even questionable they have it to spare.

That's all I know. Don't call me, call someone more likely to know the answer. We do know two things: there is a big pool of disease waiting to immigrate, so we have to talk about world-wide eradication, not just about one country. And the treatment of Hep C uses up your resistance to this sort of virus, and likely causes a re-activation of Hepatitis B if you happen to have had it in the past, as many Hep C patients undoubtedly have.

Reflections on Immortality

Notions of Immortality

When we are children, we have childish notions of immortality. Perhaps we still nourish them for lack of replacement, busying our thoughts with premature death, instead. Most of us forget the dreams of robbing candy stores or marrying a princess, and never bother to replace them. After all, everyone has to die, don't they?

So put it this way: we now have semi-realistic plans to end our lives with a thirty-year paid vacation, but what can be said about a fifty-year paid vacation, or even a hundred? Life itself is degraded by seventy years of loafing, as those who could afford it will tell you. All notions of purpose to life eventually disappear. No longer defining ourselves as soldiers and housewives; we're just cats, dogs and lice. And all our yesteryears have lighted fools the way to welcome death. As that day approaches, it will be marked by waves of awesome but fruitless literature. The Calvinist worship of work gets the last laugh of the comedy.

Subsequent generations of would-be hedonists have certainly given Calvin a hard time. Harder, in a way, than dunkings and pillories. Perhaps harder even than burning at the stake, because Calvinists had the audacity to get rich and comfortable by their effrontery. Perhaps poor and comfortable is better, and comfortable is the real goal, as Quakers were executed for advising. Once you get over the ambition to be King, what else is there?

The Stamp Tax: Highly Innovative, Much Underestimated

One of the great books about Benjamin Franklin has just emerged, and it has an interesting current Philadelphia connection. Benjamin Franklin in London fills in the eighteen years Franklin spent in Europe, with many details and insights not possible to have with three thousand miles of ocean separating his activities from his home base. In fact, it raises the question of what was really his home in his own mind. Boston claims him because he was born there, but it takes a London writer to tell us he moved to Philadelphia because of disputes over vaccination for the small pox epidemic, between his publisher brother and Cotton Mather. XX Goodwin, writer in residence at the Craven Street Ben Franklin Museum, will forever change our views about his subject. We hope he produces much more.

A word about the museum. The Craven Street house is the only Franklin residence still standing, restored with funds from Countess XX, Anthony Biddle's XXX, who unfortunately died this year. Her daughter, Charlotte Petropolis has an apartment in Philadelphia and regularly attends meetings of the Shakspere Society at the Philadelphia Club, which is itself the oldest club in America, and second oldest in the world, according to Matt Dupee, one of the local authorities on such matters, himself a member of a great many clubs around the world. To return to the original point, Goodwin is the beneficiary of this important interest by prominent Philadelphia families in our Founding Father.

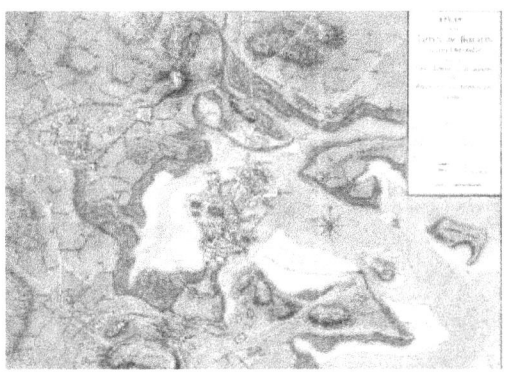

Revolutionary Boston Reconsidered

One gathers from the book that Franklin had considered himself a lifelong British subject, and from the Albany Conference of 17XX to his abject public humiliation in the "Cockpit" of Whitehall in 1775, nursed the hope that Great Britain and America would join in an empire as equals. He foresaw the growth of America, and expected the capital of the joint empire to move to America. After he returned to America, of course, the gauntlet had been thrown down, and he made it his task to enlist France on our side, bankrupting France and thus eventually provoking not one, but two national Revolutions. The French stilll think of him as their darling, but the lessons of the French Revolution taught Franklin some things he needed to know at the American Constitutional Convention of 1789. Letting others like Hamilton and Gouverneur Morris do the talking, his influence at dinners and private meetings put a stop to egalitarian babble, and established a firmly Federalist nation. His activity in London would have won him a Nobel prize instead of fairy tales about kites and keys, he was friends with Mozart and Beethoven, plus about five kings. You don't humiliate a man like that without living to regret it, and King George III certainly regretted it in his saner moments.

Which, after three paragraphs, brings us back to the Stamp Tax of 17XX. To begin with, it isn't enough to want to do something, you must figure out a way to get it done. The early 18th Century colonists had learned that smuggling and counterfeiting would frustrate any tax plan for colonies so far away with diversified economies. The oceans were filled with pirates, sometimes described as privateers, and the American coastline was thousands of miles long. Furthermore, maintaining a large British navy from the Spanish Armada to the War of the Austrian Succession required thousands of British sailors, and the Navy had been stripped down to spare expense. So naturally the idea came up to have the colonies pay for their own defense at least, but how were you going to do it, in a way you could afford to continue?

A little digging in history would probably reveal the main author of the Stamp Tax Act, but such things are often the product of staff rather than the parliamentary member who introduced them. But it ingeniously solved the empire taxation problem. You just printed up the stamps and sold them, then required the objects of taxation to have a stamp pasted somewhere on them. You still would have to worry about smuggling and counterfeiting, but the whole thing was an inexpensive way of collecting the money, and enforcing the tax. It even provided some nice patronage jobs for loyal stamp sellers.

Apparently, it was much too clever by half, since the colonists could immediately see what might be ahead of them. An uproar ensued, leading ultimately to repeal of the tax, except for a token tax on tea in order to preserve the principle. But the principle was exactly what bothered the colonists, and a tea tax wouldn't do, either. The rest is history, except I don't happen to know whose idea it really was. But I do know that

Franklin was in London at the time, and Franklin's inclinations were strongly in favor of a combined British Empire. Franklin almost lost his job in this uproar, and some of his fellow colonists may have suspected his person position on it.

TOPIC 384 Right Angle Club 2017 => BLOG 3524 After London, Ben Franklin Revisited

After London, Ben Franklin Revisited

George Goodwin appears to have written the best book I ever read, in *Benjamin Franklin in London*, which that writer in residence of the Craven Street Franklin Museum. has just produced. At least I have never read a book which proceeded to explain so much I knew puzzled me. There have been hundreds of books about Benjamin Franklin, but all of them fall back on Franklin's *Autobiography* which while surely authoritative, often omits significant details. Goodwin, concentrating on the eighteen years Franklin spent abroad, had access to many unnoticed personal papers. It was also written while Franklin was in England, where many things did not appear to need explanation to 18th Century Englishmen. And the autobiography was written for his son, who needed even less explanation. So it›s a mistake to ascribe the autobiography›s vagueness to deliberate deviousness, to say

George Goodwin

nothing of basing a whole theory of his personality on deviousness. Its hazy points now seem more attributable to his assuming his intended audience needed little explanation for what to us was seemingly left vague. And so as a first impression, Franklin himself emerges less deserving of his reputation for deceptiveness.

It occurred to me as I read it, that national opinions will change so quickly, that the transitional opinions of people like me will soon be swept aside. I am no scholar, but have read twenty or so excellent books about Benjamin Franklin, and adopted a number of fixed ideas which I will have to change. Therefore, Goodwin's achievement is in danger of becoming lost in a stampede of permanently revised views. Goodwin himself may be oblivious to his own achievement, which was probably gathered slowly after poring over heaps of primary documents, and living in a London world which needed less explaining to a Londoner. Heaven knows I am no Keats, but my place in all this can possibly aspire to his goals in the poem *On First Looking into Chapman's Homer*.

In the first place, Franklin appears to have been a staunch British subject, at least from the Albany Conference of 1754 to as late as 1774. His dream, formulated at Albany and expressed in many forms later, was that of a combined British-American empire, with its headquarters eventually to be located in America. For the largest part of his life, his attitude was not that America should be independent of Britain. It was the two nations should unite even more closely, America would inevitably grow larger, and the British Empire would become a British World. After King George

Ben Franklin In London

Join or Die

III unleashed Wedderburn to excoriate Franklin before the crowned heads of Whitehall, it all changed, of course, but it did so after a personal dispute with the King about lightning rods, where Franklin never doubted he was the world-acknowledged authority. In essence, Franklin was the inventor of electricity, but King George in effect responded, "Who do you think you are, a King?" Those weren't the words they used, but that was the sense of it. Or, considering what was at stake, the nonsense of it. Franklin had been challenged to destroy the British empire if he was so smart, and that is exactly what he set about to do.

Without editorializing a word, Goodwin allows us to read a line Franklin wrote in 1773, that King George was "perhaps the only Chance America has for obtaining soon the Address she aims at."

Franklin was not without British allies. Lord Chatham, later prime Minister, and Edmund Burke, author of "On Reconciliation With the Colonies" came very close to toppling the government over this issue. Even Lord Howe, Franklin's chess partner and brother of even-more-avid chess partner Lady Carolyn Howe, who was later designated to lead the British repression of the rebellion, is quoted as saying in 17XX, XXXXXXXX. Lord Howe's words are going to require some re-examination of his motives in abandonment of Burgoyne against direct orders, and redirection of the fleet toward Philadelphia. Frankin's response, of course, was to use the victory to sign a treaty of alliance with France.

King George III

In victorious America, of course, Franklin was celebrated for flying a kite in a rainstorm, something every schoolboy knows is too dangerous to try. It was during his time in England that Franklin performed a series of experiments which invented electricity which every physicist would agree would today win him a Nobel Prize. It made him a friend of Mozart and Beethoven, Joseph Priestley and five kings. Goodwin even restores the tarnished reputation of Peggy Stevenson.

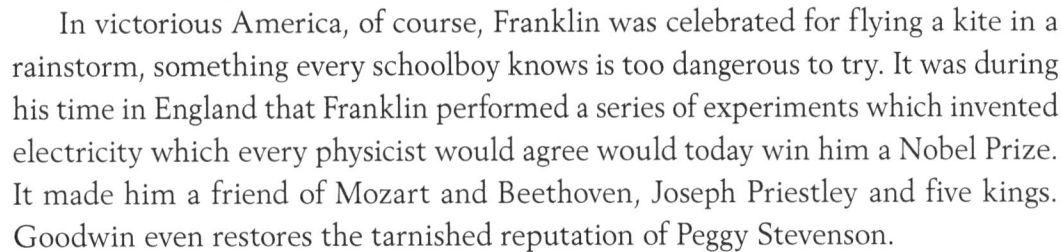
William Pitt
1st Earl of Chatham

But it isn't all for the better. Goodwin tells us Franklin didn't invent bifocals, some British optometrist did. So he raises a question, for those who are looking for it, about how many of the other American "firsts" for which he is famous, were ideas he picked up in his first trip to London in 17XX, and transported to an America eager to have what was the latest and trendiest. There are probably other innuendoes in this eminently readable but essentially scholarly work. But I missed them, and a hundred graduate students will have to put the record straight.

Innovation and Automation

The innovator is protected by patents. To some extent, the public is harmed by them, because the public wants the innovation to be cheaper. is reported to have hated patents, because they harmed the public. But less innovation harms the public, too.

Once the inventor invents an innovation, he wants to see it work. Often he employs a craftsman to make one that works, money no object. A few rich people hire artisans to make high-priced versions for various purposes, some of them noble, some just frivolous.

So, some entrepreneur risks a lot of money to build a factory, hire cheap labor if he can find it, and mass-produces a cheaper product. He hates patents, but he loves cheap labor, and he particularly hates automation, which threatens his investment.

But automation is cheaper, so it wins. The automator has to spend a lot of money to accomplish automation, but his cheaper product puts the earlier factories out of work, so they fight automation as long as they are excluded from it, but eventually surrenders. Corporations almost always defeat factories, family businesses, and artisans. Ultimately, automation, corporations and possibly inventors, tend to win. Hand craftsmen, family businesses and cheap labor tend to lose. High volume usually defeats high margins of profit,

Innovator Image

so the public usually wins, too. If the entire cycle is fast enough, the patent protects the inventor. If it's too slow, the inventor loses. It's easy to see what side each of these participants will take in the political battles, assuming the hope of profit is what motivates each one of them. The public has the votes, so at first they can do almost anything. In the long run, more innovation and cheaper prices will win public approval, but in the short run, patent impairment and job losses may hold things up.

So what is in the public interest? Job retraining and regional movement of labor are two things which come up, their expensiveness probably varies with the particular issue. But one universal good sometimes clashes with another. Is home ownership always a good thing? Are there not times when it would be better to be a renter, and move to a different employment location when your job disappears?

There are certainly times when it is better to own your own home. I finally sold my house after living in it for sixty years. The real estate agent was rueful. He saw it as his losing six sales commissions, over the years, because I did that.

Franklin and Brexit

TOPIC 384 Right Angle Club 2017 => BLOG 3578 Franklin and Brexit

In June, 2016, Great Britain voted by a million plurality, to withdraw from the European Union. The plebescite was not binding on Parliament, but Prime Minister David Cameron promptly resigned, and there remains little discussion of anything but going ahead with "Brexit". It will take at least two years to accomplish the matter, and there remains great uncertainty about the terms of separation. The British stock market took a sharp dip. Stock markets always hate uncertainty, and from the start there was little doubt Britain would experience some economic hardship, but still they went ahead with it.

Minister David Cameron

Archbishop of Canterbury

By the greatest stroke of good luck, I happened to be in London for this event. It had been barely noted in the Americana press before I left, and indeed a discussion group hadn't even put it on the agenda after my return. But let me tell you, the British public was talking about nothing else. From the lowest barmaid in a pub to the Archbishop of Canterbury, there was only one topic of conversation, and a very real understanding that Britain might well vote to leave the EU. Once the vote had been taken, of course, even the American public appreciated its significance, and its resemblance to the headlong tumult in our own political parties. Donald Trump might well win the election, and logic or rhetoric had little to do with it. Other countries, Scotland in particular, were teetering in the same direction of demonstrating how far a democracy was from a republic, when each "leader" had a million constituents. And how well the public appreciated the tendency of elected representatives to forget who elected them. Or else, in more rational moments, to appreciate how difficult it is for elected representatives to communicate with constituents.

To go on with this insight for a moment, my Washington daughter tells me Democrat congressmen are required to spend thirty-six hours every week in a call center, soliciting campaign funds; where do they find time to legislate? But the central background reflection I happened to have about Brexit was how enduring the political split apparently was between the Whigs and the Tories. This thought came to me from one of the real reasons I was in London, to visit Ben Franklin's imposing rowhouse on Craven Street, fifty feet from the National Museum on Piccadilly. Franklin lived there for most of eighteen years, in a style quite different from the two-penny loaf of bread in Philadelphia. He was personal friends with five kings, Voltaire, Mozart and Beethoven, as well as Priestly, Lavoisier, and Hume. Townsend may indeed have passed the Stamp Act, but he invited Franklin to spend the weekend at his hundred-room castle. The neighbors on Craven Street easily recognized the carriage of the Prime Minister when he came to call on Franklin on Craven Street. From the

Ben Franklin London Townhome

King George III

point of view of this social set, the uproar over the colonies was whether England should conquer them and send their raw materials to British factories (the Tory view), or should instead colonize them with Brits, give them the vote, and rule the world as a commonwealth (the Whig view). Naturally, Franklin supported the Whigs, but his loyalty to his good friend George III, never wavered until 1775. And then, lightening struck St. Paul's Cathedral.

Quite logically, the King asked Franklin's advice. The King however insisted on a brass ball on the top of the church. Franklin resisted, saying a spire was much more effective. We don't have the exact words exchanged, but essentially the King said he was going to have his way, while Franklin in effect asked him who he thought he was talking to. In those days, far less direct wording was needed to give offense on such a central issue of the king having the last word whenever he wanted. It is intimated the King suggested to Weddeburn he should take care of the issue for him, and within a few weeks Franklin was subjected to public humiliation in the cockpit at Whitehall, threatened with arrest, and fled to America to start the war. I had never heard this story, before.

The point it leaves me with is not that Franklin lost his cool and should have known better than to express his opinion. Rather, it is the reflection that never before had a king been challenged on his divine opinion on any subject. Just think of the shock this must have caused him, to have to realize this was the first snowflake in a blizzard. With the Enlightenment and the Industrial Revolution, the world was going to be full of experts, who could make a fool of any king by disagreeing with him in public. This particular king was able to have his way, no matter what, but the day was soon approaching when any science editor, any university professor, and ultimately every barmaid in a pub, could pontificate to the Pontiff.

TOPIC 384 Right Angle Club 2017 => BLOG 2663 Honoring the Fallen

Honoring the Fallen

Two of Philadelphia's most honored institutions, Quakerism and the First City Troop, are in conflict.
The roarin' Twenties, just after the First World War, were a time when we seemed to change conventional attitudes about Society. But in many ways the convulsive changes of the Twenties were merely a

process of facing up to what we already knew. In retrospect, many of the deeply emotional conflicts of that time, now seem entirely bearable. Scott Fitzgerald's most ponderous statement, the one that says "The test of a first-rate intelligence is the ability to hold two opposing ideas in mind at the same time and still retain the ability to function," reduces itself to the trivial agonies of loving two girls at a time, or choosing to stop smoking when you always knew you shouldn't start. Just about the only instance I can think of, where two deeply loved Philadelphia institutions are in seriously troubling conflict, are the First City Troop, and Quakerism. The matter came to mind at the Right Angle Club, when a Philadelphia Trooper who simply radiated the honorable dedications of upper-class Philadelphia gentlemen, meekly described his dedication to restoring the crumbling monuments of bravely fallen comrades. The monuments he finds and restores at great personal expense are not merely war heroes, although one suspects that is the root of it. The gravestones and monuments crumbling in the dust are markers of heroes of our civilization generally. But we do forget what we owe them, and neglect their monuments.

F. Scott Fitzgerald

Fourth Street Meetinghouse

Although the dominant Quakers of Philadelphia's early days are now reduced to a handful of practicing believers, almost every educated Philadelphian knows those beliefs pretty well. The early Friends did not even sympathize with carving their names on their tombstones. If you visit the Fourth Street Meetinghouse, you will be told that forty thousand bodies have been buried on the grounds, but only two graves have tombstones. The worship of grave markers, you will softly be told, is idolatry. The goal of a funeral should not be to mourn a death, but to celebrate a life well-lived. And although the custom of gravestones has reasserted itself, it does not take long to be gently reminded that keeping alive the memories of one war's atrocities, can eventually lead to more wars. We recently have seen wars in Bosnia and Kosovo being fought over Thirteenth Century grievances which might better be forgotten. Some of this comes from immigration over three thousand miles of ocean, but the effect is the same. I have no idea even what nationality my own 13th Century ancestors might have fought for, and I doubt if the world would be improved if I found out and sought to wreak vengeance for the inevitable atrocities.

But unless one is determined to denounce anything at all admirable about everything our society does to defend itself -- and there are some who go that far -- it is necessary to make a sad concession to force in successful governance. The 18th Century Quakers perhaps seldom acknowledged the need for occasional force as a condition for leadership, but they watched their children drift away from the religion, once they absorbed the lesson. Even those who choose conscientious objection for themselves, must occasionally acknowledge the debt they owe to those who do answer the call of force, and knowingly fail to survive it.

Philadelphia First City Troop

There simply is no choice but to honor both sides of this issue, both permanently and side by side. There are some who can't, and in various ways fail to retain the ability to function. As in many of his more

Society of Friends

juvenile pronouncements, Fitzgerald does go much too far with assessing all the rest of Philadelphia as having less than first-rate intelligence. Philadelphians generally have at least a taste of the experience of holding these two opposing ideas-- the City Troop and the Society of Friends -- in mind at the same time, with approval for both. And generally seeming somewhat improved for having made the struggle.

Michael Dell, the Millionaire Teen-ager

Michael Dell

Happy Birthday, Mike.
    The Franklin Institute gives out an annual award for business innovations, and a few years ago it was given to Michael Dell. The banquet is very splendid and well-attended by people willing to pay high prices. So, it happened that the founder of Dell Computers was wandering around the dinner table where I was seated. Being a gregarious sort of guy, he introduced himself and told his story.

As he relates it, his mother gave him a new IBM portable computer for his 19th birthday. So, he took it upstairs to his bedroom along with a screwdriver, and took it all apart.

What he discovered annoyed his mother, but intrigued the birthday guests. Every single part of the computer was composed of articles obtained from other manufacturers. So he got in touch with these parts makers, and asked for their prices. His discovery was that he could assemble a duplicate computer for half the price his mother had paid. One thing led to another, and he was soon producing Dell computers for much less than IBM was selling them. Naturally, there is a market for such a product, particularly if they were sold without middle-men, mail-order. And in the course of a short time, he became a billionaire, IBM got out of the business, and it was all his.

Dell Computer

As is so common with stories like this, he eventually went bust, and was soon engaged in new adventures. But he took his screwdriver to other tables, and we never did hear about those later exploits.

TOPIC 384 Right Angle Club 2017 => BLOG 3761 Azaleas and Rhodedendrons at Tyler Arboretum

Azaleas and Rhodedendrons at Tyler Arboretum

All azaleas are rhodedendrons, but all rhodedendrons are not azaleas. Philadelphia has more arboretums than anywhere else, probably dating from the days when Quakers frowned on aesthetic entertainments, but held lots and lots of land. Curiously, azaleas are a Quaker thing (remember Swarthmore College and Friends Hospital), while anti-azalea feelings are growing among non-Quakers. It all has to do with bugs.

Tyler Arboretum

Azaleas flourish in Korea, where the hills are covered with pink bushes in the spring, and Quaker merchant ships brought them home to sell as curiosities. Both Korea and Philadelphia are on the 40th parallel, so azaleas flourish in both places. But Japan and Korea escaped the glaciers, so their plant life was sort of isolated and unique until inter- continental merchants came along. The rest of the world therefore contained few natural predators, and they grew unhindered, here. Generally speaking, azaleas are an East Coast phenomenon; it is not uncommon for midwestern visitors to exclaim they never saw them before, although it is true rhodedendrons love acid soil, and rather suffer from the alkaline midwestern soil left over from the seashells of the ancient central sea bottom.

Azaleas flourish in Korea

On the other hand, there is a growing anti-azalea craze among avid gardeners, taking the form of pro-nativist feelings much like R vs. D. The recent hatred of imported flowers reflect a reaction to "invasive" weeds brought here by importing other globalized products and dumping them along the banks and shorelines. The common denominator is lack of native weed enemies to both the globalized weeds, and azaleas, which caused a withering of the bugs which eat the plants, and in turn are eaten by birds. So this discovery by the University of Delaware took root in Mount Cuba, the duPont estate which is exclusively and consciously planted with nativist plants, and promoted by socially prominent families who like birds more than show-gardens -- and enjoy tax benefits from botany favored land preservation.

Rhododendron

This results in an alarming pressure to encourage Philadelphia's many arboreta to play down the showy azaleas they formerly favored, making enemies out of friends. It seemingly pits those who love birds against those barbarians who love gardens. It seems unnecessary for the bird lovers to attack the innocent gardeners, when the focus might be turned against the bugs, where many fewer would take offense. Just think of the possibilities of Girl Scouts taking up the cause of bug hybridization, running around the countryside with glass jars to capture likely natural predators to the bugs which plant- predators favor to promote the right kind of birds. That way, we might have our birds -- and preserve our azaleas too. Meanwhile breeding the right sort of bug no one would notice, or inhibiting the wrong sort of bug if that proves the easier path to follow. Maybe Dow Chemicals could make a fortune with a selective bug-killer spray, and keep the former duPont company from entering this dispute between seemingly natural friends.

Philadelphia Arboreta

TOPIC 384 Right Angle Club 2017 => BLOG 3819 Artificial Intelligence

Artificial Intelligence

James Marsh

Earlier this year, the Franklin Inn Club and the Right Angle Club held lectures on the same subject (Artificial Intelligence) on two successive luncheons. The Franklin Inn was addressed by a member, Jim Marsh a former engineer, and the Right Angle by a member who was formerly in charge of investing the retirement portfolio of the Dupont Company. Essentially they said the same thing about two apparently unconnected industries. Artificial Intelligence is rapidly acquiring new abilities, and it's soon going to revolutionize the whole world.

At least, judging by the speed things are changing in the computer world, unreported advances will soon fill in the gaps which will make dramatic change inevitable. That's slightly different, and much of it is beyond American control. The central advance is for computers to utilize massive extensions of their present abilities, enabling them to test huge new conjectures rapidly by writing code for computers without depending on human innovation. Machines have a bigger, more permanent memory, and can test and implement wide varieties of new ideas beyond human abilities to keep up. That is, unless human innovation blows us up first.

Appparently, trucks are apparently just on the edge of loading and pulling out of a loading block, and driving across the country--without a driver and without an accident. Human autos will be greatly reduced in number, possible replaced by driverless taxis. Fewer potholes, fewer street repairs. People out of work, nothing to tax.

What is AI?

The stock broker probably had a longer viewpoint than the engineer. so both of them may be right, at slightly different times. Artificial intelligence will increase supply, and also increase demand, but at different times. That will generate two collisions, one with supply in excess and the other with demand in excess, but at different times. So, in the short run we have lower prices, and in the long run we have greater growth. Or even *vice versa* , a crash followed by a boom, or possibly a boom followed by a crash, and it doesn't much matter whether it if triggered by crude oil prices, or the price of silk stockings.

How soon? Ah, that's the question. Right now people are behaving as though they think it may be two or three years. That may be true, but it seldom is true that people anticipate the future accurately. More often, what everybody knows, isn't worth knowing.

TOPIC 384 Right Angle Club 2017 => BLOG 3804 Quakers and Idolatry

Quakers and Idolatry

Early Quakers were so opposed to idolatry, they wouldn''t allow tombstones. There are about forty thousand bodies buried in Philadelphia's Quaker Meetinghouse grounds at Fourth and Arch Streets, which contain only two tombstones. The yellow fever epidemics of the era account for much of that, but it's nevertheless a striking portrayal of early Quaker aversion to anything resembling idolatry. It underlines this attitude by sharp contrast with more recent uproars about desecrating statues of Confederate generals in public spaces of the Old South, which even Robert E. Lee objected to constructing. They led plausibly to erecting and then defacing Union generals in Northern states as well; since it seemed natural for statue-desecration to evolve into an equal-opportunity demonstrations. A little primitive perhaps, but even-handed.

Philadelphia›s Quaker Meetinghouse

Worshiping graven images has a long history. You needn't be a public-statue expert to remember the terracotta Chinese soldiers are two thousand years old, and the Egyptian pyramids are even older. The chariot horses over the Brandenburg Gate make a stronger illustration of the idea, intertwined over the shorter length of Western civilization. Although carvings might be older, we also have a reasonably accurate history of the bronze statues of these horses. The technique evolved with different proportions of copper and tin, with other metals sometimes added, but the underlying idea is to make a hollow bronze statue, giving the appearance of a much heavier solid bronze one, apparently originating in the Greek islands off the coast of Turkey in the second Century. There were in fact two such statues, with different subsequent

The Fourth Crusade

Frederick the Great

histories. The Fourth Crusade was the one where Western European Christian Crusaders invaded Constantinople the main eastern Christian capital, never getting to the Holy Land. Even if they started with good intentions, Christians were content to carry off Christian booty, including the bronze horses. One set was sent to Venice and the other set got to the Christians in Southern France.

Frederick the Great put one set in the center of Berlin. In time, Napoleon took both statues to Paris, but later returned them. The one in Berlin, or perhaps copies of it eventually came to symbolize Nazi Germany, but later Checkpoint Charlie. The details of these conquests and adventures are not not of much consequence today, leaving only the central point that someone conquered someone else, and God must love the victor. The main point became victory, dogmas have been forgotten. Only the Quakers seem to be willing to mention another main point: Thousands of people died for these statues, but very few tourists could now tell you why. The Quakers reached a conclusion we might reconsider. Pulverize all statues and churches, thus saving the world from future grief. Since the Quakers also were first to free the slaves but later mostly disapproved of the Civil War, the irony was not lost on them. But most of their grandchildren reversed the assessment. It's too early to say how another generation will be persuaded to feel.

During the War against Nazi Germany, my uncle was General Lucius Clay's room-mate, and the two of them were appointed to oversee de-Nazification of the defeated Germans by a third Pennsylvania Dutchman, Dwight Eisenhower. The concept was devised by Henry Morganthau, then Secretary of the Treasury, in a famous letter urging a program to make Germany into an agricultural nation "for a thousand years". Accordingly, my father's brother oversaw the public burning of tons of postage stamps containing swastikas, plus every photograph of Adolph Hitler the Army could locate, along with similar symbols of the Third Reich. Nearly eighty years have passed since then -- essentially two generations, but it still remains illegal to possess such documents. Evidently, a sense of vengefulness so regularly outlasts its provocation, that passing the grievance on to children is usually hard to justify.

General Lucius Clay

TOPIC 384 Right Angle Club 2017 => BLOG 3760 Fraud and Abuse in Medicare and Other Government Programs

Fraud and Abuse in Medicare and Other Government Programs

Medicare and Medicaid spend 10% on services which were never or unnecessarily performed. Fraud and abuse currently total about $100 billion per year.

Fraud and Abuse is a common debater's ploy to avoid serious reform in government programs. Just eliminate that cost which everyone would deplore, and some pesky reform proposal won't be necessary, is the implication. Usually everyone acknowledges this unanswerable way of playing on anti-government voter sentiment, because taxes are just the cost of self-government. Other governments may be crooked, but Americans can be trusted, and so forth. So it becomes useful to have some reasonably accurate estimate of just how serious this issue really is. To make short work of it, this is really a serious issue.

Fraud and Abuse

The U.S. Government Accountability Office (GAO) had been keeping data on itself for some time, and now reduces it to a simple graph. Fraud is twice as bad as it was eight years ago, and that figure was twice as bad as thirteen years ago. We seem to be talking about 100 billion dollars a year, hardly small change or a thing of the past. Medicare paid out about 600 billion dollars in 2016, and Medicaid another 360 billion; the fiscal 2017 amount will surely total over $1 trillion. Using GAO figures, 100 billion dollars were spent on government health claims "that were not delivered, were unnecessary or were otherwise erroneous". Since Medicare is only half of total medical care billed by essentially the same approach, why would anyone assume a single payer system would save money? Remember, none of these estimates includes anything at all to run the program itself, so it is entirely reasonable to suppose a single-payer system could cost 15% of $2 trillion, or $300 billion dollars per year just to transfer the money. Expenses of that sort approach $1000 per year for every man, woman and child, whether he gets sick or not, in order to shift $9000, mostly to other people. Such drastic proposals justify examination of wholly different approaches.

U.S. Government Accountability Office (GAO)

TOPIC 384 Right Angle Club 2017 => BLOG 3758 The Lawsuit That Ate Philadelphia

The Lawsuit That Ate Philadelphia

Other cities want to attract Silicon Valley, Philadelphia drove it away.

Hastings Griffin ("Haste") died last week in his nineties. The Orpheus Club put on a concert at his memorial service, and probably the Squash world put on something, because he was the reigning world champion for his age group. And his wife was there in all her glory, having married and outlived three men, all of whom were roommates at Princeton; among women, that's a champion on a different level. I knew Haste as a fellow member of the Shakspere Society, where his booming voice was an arresting feature, particularly when you knew his motorcycle was parked outside, ready for the 30-mile trip home at night to his home near Valley Forge. But I knew him to be most famous as the lawyer who was on the losing side of a lawsuit which cost Philadelphia the whole computer industry.

F. Hastings Griffin

As a matter of fact, I am very friendly with Ben Heintzen, the lawyer on the winning side of the same case. So, over a period of years I was able to piece together the main facts of the case, checking remarks

John Mauchly (on Left) a nd J. Presper Eckert

from one side against the recollections of the other. First of all, the computer as we know it was assembled by Mauchly and Eckert, on the faculty of the University of Pennsylvania. Eckert had patented it, but the University had a rule that patents of the faculty belonged to the university. Unfortunately for that position, all of the money was government money. Right there, you have the makings of a big lawsuit, but there was much more. Ben Heitzen had discovered a paper by a midwestern professor, Iowa I believe, who seems to have put the patent in the public domain by publishing the main substance of it, or what lawyers contended was the essence of the case. Furthermore, the case had many plaintiffs and defendants, working more or less together, but under the team leadership of Sperry Rand for the defendants, and Honeywell for the plaintiffs. The case dragged on for more than eight years, to the delight of the law firms and dismay of the Judge, who had been heard to growl that he didn,t want to spend the rest of his life listening to this same case. All a losing lawyer had to do was wait for the verdict to tell you who won, and then file an appeal that the Judge had acted in prejudice. Furthermore, the Judge expressed the opinion that IBM wanted to mass produce computers, whereas Sperry was really only in the "patent infringement business." Somebody said that, perhaps it was the Judge. Well, there's more.

It happens that Sperry Rand had round holes in their punch-cards, and IBM had square holes. The hanging chad issue became famous in the Gore-Bush presidential election, and you would suppose square holes would have more of a tendency to hang their chads than round ones, but it was actually the other way around. It seemed so to Sperry Rand, too, so they finally hired IBM engineers to tell them what the matter was, and those IBM engineers were hanging around while the trial was going on. They must have picked up the gossip in the lunch room, and reported back to Tom Watson at IBM something like, "Do you know what these people are doing with computers?"

Sperry Rand Building

So they were given orders to stretch out the hanging chad matter and see what else they could learn. When Watson heard more, he told his lawyers to ask what Sperry wanted in return for letting IBM out of the lawsuit, and the answer came back,"Ten million dollars". To which Watson replied, "Pay them immediately, because we are going to mass-produce those things." At that time, there were only a handful of computers, all doing such things as calculating field artillery aiming instructions. So Watson was essentially betting his whole company on success.At that time, General Electric, RCA, Sperry, Burroughs, Honeywell and others were in Philadelphia, trying to imitate what they had heard the machines were capable of, so it was not a sure-fire gamble at all, but it was certainly successful in moving computers to upstate New York, and eventually to Silicon Valley.

Since half of this story comes from Griffin, let me reconcile a point that came up at his funeral. One of his partners heard him boast he had never lost a case, and when challenged on it, replied that it didn't matter what the jury decided, it was the judge who must approve the size of the settlement. His claim was based on getting settlements down to much less

UNIVAC (Sperry Rand) Unimatic terminal

than the client was afraid it might be, and was therefore persuaded he had been lucky. Well, in this case it was a little different. The chief lawyer of the firm took the case away from Griffin and carried it himself. Shortly later, Griffin was heard to shout at the boss, "You are going to lose this case!". The next morning he was standing at the airport, next to the President of Sperry Rand. The President came close and asked him, "How do you think this case is going?"

To which Haste replied, "Well, sir, you'll have to ask my boss."

TOPIC 384 Right Angle Club 2017 => BLOG 3486 Suggested Additions.

Suggested Additions

Soon after the release date of the first edition of this book, an article appeared in the *Wall Street Journal* by Lanhee J. Chen and James C. Capretta of Stanford University, entitled *Instead of Obamacare: Giving Healthcare to the People*. The authors were in general sympathy with the Health Savings Account approach, and made three other suggestions with which I more-or-less agree. But they add a fourth which makes me unhappy :

Lanhee J. Chen

1. Continuous Coverage Protection. They rightly notice many mandatory auto insurance recipients take out insurance, pay a single month's premium, during which time they obtain their drivers license. And then no further payments are made for the insurance. The authors propose higher premiums for those who do the same thing with healthcare insurance, but presumably waive the higher cost if insurance is continued for a full year. There are many people who are suspicious of making anything mandatory, but if it's mandatory, it's unfair to allow obvious loopholes of this sort to persist.

2. Medicaid Reform. The two commenting authors are evidently aware of the unsatisfactory quality of many state Medicaid programs, and propose splitting Medicaid into two parts, one for able-bodied adults and their children, and another for the disabled and elderly. Essentially, this is a rewording of high-risk pools, partially achieved by splitting Medicaid from federal plans. While this division might mesh more easily with existing workers and their families in the event of universal coverage (under a single-payer system), by itself it would not address much else.

   A more useful split would be between inpatients and outpatients. That would match Medicare A and B, as well as the underlying Blue-Cross/Blue Shield organization of paperwork. Moreover, splitting helpless inpatients from ambulatory outpatients could surprisingly enable the marketplace to influence inpatient costs. Since a large number of outpatient and inpatient services are identical, it would establish a comparison framework for approximating inpatient to outpatient prices through a two-step market mechanism, which ultimately approximates market prices. For those inpatient services which have no outpatient match, a relative value system would provide a more stable way to set prices for the remainder of helpless inpatients. Doing this would close a loophole commonly employed to cost-shift inpatient costs to the outpatient area, resulting in vast confusion between two pricing systems for identical procedures. Hospital administrators would resist losing the ability to shift prices, so ultimately this is an argument about who is to dominate prices, the consumers or the providers. The "market" is a compromise between the two.

3. Medicare Reform. The main reason Medicare is often preferred to Medicaid is, it is potentially available to everyone regardless of income. But Medicare itself is 50% subsidized by the general taxpayer. No wonder Medicare doesn't need to mandate coverage. Effectively Medicare is subsidized more generously than Medicaid, and thus is the main source of healthcare deficits. You might subsidize Medicaid more generously, or you could apply a 50% subsidy to a single payer system. Either way will cost more, not less. Speaking politically, it is a question of whether you wish to offend the elderly Medicare patients, or the younger indigent ones. Essentially, Congress has already chosen sides once, and is unlikely to change its preference for current voters rather than potential ones. Finally, there remains one suggestion in the article which does make me uncomfortable, because of what it fails to say.

(4.) Retaining Employer Coverage. It still costs less to provide health insurance for employees, than to pay them wages and let them buy the same health insurance with what is left. Employers are therefore better off giving the health insurance as a gift, even though recent inflation has held back wages more than health costs. Presumably this anomaly would not survive tax reform, because employer-basing has turned into one big tax dodge.

But if it should survive, it presents the alternative to rectify the injustice to the other half of (small business) employees, whose employers usually can not donate the coverage and then make it up at a spuriously higher corporate tax rate. Persisting eighty years after World War II which created the pretext, this is an unnecessary reminder of the many irregularities in the tax code. However, a one-line amendment to the HSA Law would suffice to extend the same tax exemption to outsiders, allowing other issues to remain dormant. This simple amendment would **permit the premiums of a catastrophic health plan to be paid by the Health Savings Account itself**, thereby extending its own tax shelter to HSA owners, at less additional commotion to the Treasury than full exemption. The present inflation distortion should not be missed as an opportunity to restore fairness, which almost everyone now recognizes to be nothing but a lobbying plum.

James C. Capretta

TOPIC 384 Right Angle Club 2017 => BLOG 3497 H.I.V., AIDS, and the Law

H.I.V., AIDS, and the Law
New blog 2016-03-06 00:14:30 description

We had a meeting in March at our new quarters in the Pyramid Club, conventional in all respects except members were urged to bring a female guest. It was extremely well attended, which probably improved the food somewhat. Come to think of it, the jokes were cleaned up a little bit, too. But because the central subject was also doubly controversial, covering both the subject of AIDS and the trial bar, I omit all names from this report, in an effort to maintain neutrality on the specific case matter, while discussing the general subject of conflict between the bar and the medical profession.

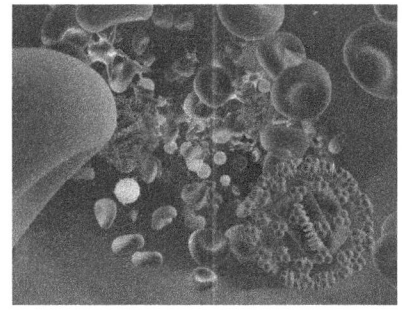
AIDS

The case under discussion took place in 1987, so it is important to remember the state of knowledge about A.I.D.S at that moment. Nobody knew for certain what caused the disease, or how to treat it. It was universally fatal, and seemed to be contagious in some way. At least, it seemed to originate in Africa among primates, and when brought to America through Haiti, seemed to concentrate in male homosexuals, although not exclusively. It had a peculiar concentration of brain tumors, and a strange proclivity for yeast infections of the lung. At first, there was no test for this condition, but over the course of fifteen years went from a totally mysterious and ominous condition, to a curable disease. Indeed a largely preventable one, caused by a virus of the retro-virus variety, for which a highly reliable blood test was devised, and a quite effective treatment. Comparatively few Americans now die of AIDS, now called H.I.V. infection, although the disease continues to spread devastation in countries with more primitive medical systems. I hope I have given a fair summary of one of the most rapid investigations into a new complex disease in all of medical history.

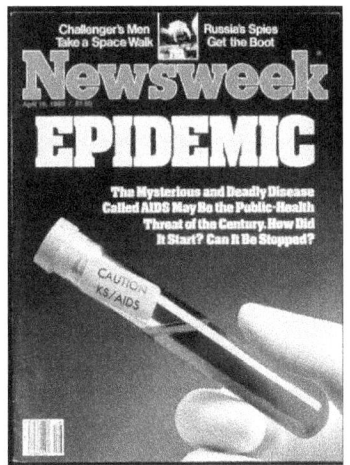
AIDS knowledge

Enormous amounts of money were poured into research in this condition, probably greatly stimulated by public pressure generated by the gay community, and others.

The lawyer who presented the case to us was called into the matter by a client who had been fired because he had the condition. How much the client, defendant law firm, or plaintiff lawyer knew about the condition at the time was not elaborated. But it surely was incomplete, quite possibly quite rudimentary. Expert witnesses were consulted, although it is not clear how much they could have known at the time, either. In any event, it was determined the patient was still able to work at the time he was fired. The state of the law on the subject was equally fuzzy in 1987, and the basis of the claim was an infringement of disability fairness, or some legal variation of this language. He wasn't disabled, was the basis for the court's decision, and in a sense that was true.

"Philadelphia"

However, a question was raised from the audience as to whether the issue of contagiousness in the workplace was raised, and the plaintiff lawyer replied it was not; perhaps his impromptu response was somehow inaccurate. However, taking matters at face value, it is possible to imagine the executive of the firm was alarmed by the possibility that other members of the firm would resign rather than subject themselves to the hazard of contracting the disease themselves, thereby destroying the firm. Even so, dismissing the employee seems excessive; he might have been given a medical leave of absence, or some other means of preventing spread of the disease might have been devised. But the point is the firm had a legitimate concern, and probably could not be sure of reassuring the other employees in a scientific way; an unwarranted panic could not be prevented by legitimate scientific arguments available at the time. That the firm chose a cumbersome unfair way of protecting themselves is not completely surprising, any more than a guaranteed way to escape a fire in a theater is even now available, except by not going to the theater.

Louis Pasteur

Until Louis Pasteur discovered the germ theory of disease around 1880, epidemics of contagious disease devastated whole communities for thousands of years. Thucydides described an epidemic in ancient Athens hundreds of years B.C., and even today we are not entirely certain what that disease really was. Since that time, society has developed legal and management techniques of mild utility, since the courts have had to devise some sort of order out of this panic situation. But whether the best scientific approach takes fifteen years to emerge, or centuries, the court decision has to be made on principles which may seem wrong-headed in retrospect. Once the scientific facts are firmly established, the process of undoing unfortunate precedents has to be commenced during which, further blunderings may take place. Finally, the courts and the medical profession may come to agree on the best approach, but it can take a long time. Since presumably there will be future outbreaks of future unknown diseases, I have a suggestion.

Discussions between the two professions ought to be held, to devise a mechanism of appeal to a special scientific court devoted to the problem which arises. The appeals court should refrain from issuing legal opinions until the scientific matter seems to have settled down, but a scientific opinion about the current state of scientific understanding might be quite welcome. At least the provisional court would know its decision would have to be provisional, anticipating later revisions of the law which undo judicial precedents set in a time when only expediency was possible. The situation already exists of the Courts of Equity, designed to meet situations where injustice obviously exists, but no law can adequately address it.

TOPIC 384 Right Angle Club 2017 => BLOG 3487 Exit Strategy: Medicare as the First Pearl in the HSA Necklace

Exit Strategy: Medicare as the First Pearl in the HSA Necklace

Placing a termination point for Health Savings Accounts was originally occasioned by recognizing the overlap created in 1965 by Medicare for everyone. At the time, it seemed pointless to be covered by Health Savings Accounts in addition to Medicare, and there was confusion with Health Spending Accounts with their "use it or lose it" features. Pouring remaining HSA surpluses into a regular IRA retirement fund, seems in retrospect the most effective way to create some incentive to save as much as you can in the Accounts. You couldn't lose it, and might well need it. To a certain degree, the size of the resulting retirement package is determined by the frugality of the individual client during his whole medical lifetime long before, but also during, the time he is on Medicare.

He would, however not be in the position of needing to do that, if he had been born earlier. The subscriber to an HSA could continue to deposit extra tax-exempt money in the roll-over IRA for his retirement, giving the appearance of laundering it. Unfortunately, he would first have to drop out of the healthcare benefits, so he would lose the laundered tax exemption for health benefits on withdrawal. You would now have to view the extended tax exemption as repairing that unintended inequity. As Medicare began to be less generous, there were increasing gaps in coverage, and there may be many more in the future.

In what follows, we extend the retirement roll-over idea to several other medical entitlements without suggesting it be required as a universal rule. The time-honored old approach was to use an insurance surplus to reduce costs by recycling its surplus, but there are other things to consider. The first would be to imagine a theoretical sharp drop in the cost of Medicare, itself. Since 80% of Medicare is now spent on five or ten diseases, the possibility of a sudden cheap cure of one of those diseases is raised. The astonishing savings in the cost of strokes and heart attacks, created by taking a daily aspirin tablet -- shows what it might be possible to imagine as happening again. Not to promise, but to imagine.

On the other hand, it is also possible to imagine less desirable priorities getting into the competition for such a financial windfall. Confronted with the issue, the average person would likely suspect such a windfall might as likely pay for aircraft carriers as Medicare deficits. But another opinion would emerge, and should be the default position. The Medicare program and its members had experienced the unexpected -- and expensive -- consequence of more protracted retirement than they planned on (five times as expensive, by one estimate). A more just assignment of such windfall would be to pay for the extra-long retirement cost it had provoked. If other emergencies seemed more pressing at the time, they could always be given priority on the money, but by default Medicare should first pay for its own consequences. In fact, nothing of the sort occurred.

In a sense, President Obama later created the same political problem for himself with the original budget for Obamacare. He did not need to make any speeches directing attention to the diversion of Medicare money to help pay for Obamacare costs, because plenty of Republican opponents were studying the budget. And plenty of Republicans remembered Richard Nixon's advice, "Watch what I do, don't listen to what I say." Having spoken to many groups of retirees about healthcare financing, I am acutely aware that retirees are watchful for any move to strip Medicare funds for Obamacare's benefit. It's about their highest priority.

And indeed their anxiety would be heightened by discovering Medicare is already 50% subsidized by general taxation, and then unsustainably maintained by borrowing money (selling US Treasury bonds) to foreign countries like China. And still more to the point, medical costs have been and will continue to migrate from working age people to retirement age people in the future. Just about everyone who dies right now, dies at Medicare expense. Even more than that, the effect of medical science has tended to eliminate terminal medical costs for people under 65, shifting them to people who get sick when they are over 65. It can be predicted a major cause of future Medicare cost increases, compared with the cost of living, lies in this shift of disease cost to the elderly. So it's a little hard to project whether Medicare costs will go up or go down, even if the cost of illness remains the same.

Recipients will change insurance compartments. Many attempts have been made to shift Medicare costs to the non-sick working population, such as through the payroll tax deduction and hospital internal cost-shifting, but the trend continues. A more sophisticated thing for the retirees to worry about, is the instability of a system which depends for its financing on that one-third of the population who are at work

-- but who are themselves becoming progressively more healthy -- to support the medical finances of the other two thirds of the population, who are sick.

Taken in summary, there exists a great political opportunity for both political parties to put a stop to this "third rail of politics" talk. And to amend the Medicare Law immediately to provide that any declines in Medicare costs be immediately transferred to Social Security, for the purpose of paying for further increases in longevity. That provision should not cost much for some time to come. But the incentive it would give to the retirees to reduce their health expenditures might be considerable. Just as the comparable position Health Savings Accounts achieved, once Medicare coverage was attained.

But its real benefit might be tested on that fateful day in the future. The day you pick up the morning newspaper and discover someone has cured cancer.

TOPIC 384 Right Angle Club 2017 => BLOG 3506 Getting Started

Getting Started
New blog 2016-03-29 18:52:39 description

So it's simple to get started, although any obvious modifications like periodic payroll deductions, are between you and your vendor.

To repeat: you choose a high deductible health insurance plan which conforms to regulations. Since they vary in price and service, you are advised to shop around, probably starting with the Internet, or the personnel department of your employer, or your friends. At the moment, a number of features are fixed by the Affordable Care Act, so price and service are really the main issues.

Then, having identified a (high-deductible) insurer and an HSA vendor (perhaps a bank or investment adviser), you are free to switch later, but in the long run you are looking for more-or-less permanent relationships.

You now presumably have your health insurance policy, with a Christmas saving fund arrangement attached. Don't sign anything until you are satisfied with the answer to this question, "How much income can I expect and how much freedom do I have to invest in total market stock index funds, when and if I choose to?"

If you get evasive answers, you might silently plan to sign up, but plan to keep on looking for a better deal to switch to later. At first, it might not matter, but over time you need to find the best arrangement. A debit card attachment is nice. Big vendors are reassuring, but they tend to be inflexible. Bear in mind, there isn't much in it for your advisor unless you keep renewing for a long time, so if you persist, your will probably get an answer. If persistence doesn't work, the outlook for a favorableanswer, however, is dim.

So you might suddenly improve the atmosphere if you offer plans to deposit the maximum allowable immediately, because a lot of obstacles will likely be waived. Keep that up for as long as you can, at least until minimum balance requirements are fulfilled. If you can't manage it, then use the Christmas fund approaches of payroll deductions and income penalties for as long as you have to, but remember your counterparty really must somehow be paid, even though he always remains a counterparty. What about the retirement income features? You probably don't have to worry about retirement for many years, although it is always wise to check occasionally to see how income compares with the competition. As things now stand, you needn't do anything until you become eligible for Medicare, except keep score between your arrangement and others, reacting appropriately to differences. As the time approaches, you will probably find you have lots of choices of retirement plans, so don't be in a rush to freeze that option.

Whether it is explicit or not, let's say you have done everything necessary for both a health insurance plan and, following that, a retirement plan. The retirement plan will have no money in it until you shift it there from the health insurance plan, replaced with Medicare. There are penalties for early withdrawals, but they can be made, if you must. So to summarize, there's a little nuisance when you start, and another bit when Medicare looms. But essentially the Health Savings Account is on auto-pilot if you keep funding it, and events continue to demonstrate you are getting the maximum available return.

That completes the first section of this book. It all may be a little hard to understand, but it's easy to do. The last part of the book is devoted to what else you and Congress might think about, to build additional features on top of this foundation. Most of these extensions would greatly enhance the finances of you and the rest of the country, but all of them must be debated in minute detail before implementation. And all of them require major legislation to be smooth and workable. The Health and Retirement Savings Account as it stands might use a few easy amendments, but it already has most of its kinks worked out. It's already reached the point where the claim can be made it's a whole lot better than any other term insurance plan.

One by one, let's examine the potential multi-year improvements to be debated, so at least you understand where all this might take you.

TOPIC 384 Right Angle Club 2017 => BLOG 3513 Looking a Gift Horse in the Mouth

Looking a Gift Horse in the Mouth
New blog 2016-04-06 16:44:14 description

The Progressive Era lasted several decades, some say it still continues. Around 1910, the Progressive Era, reacting to the Gilded Age which preceded it, started doing painful things in the best interest of the individual, like the graduated income tax, the War to End Wars, and employer-based insurance.

Regardless of originator or date, employer based health insurance was imported as an idea from Germany in the nineteen-teens, getting started in the nineteen twenties, and becoming the prevailing standard by World War II. Although control later shifted from employers toward government

Progressive Era

during this period, Harry Truman was unable to move it further. It was only in 1965 that government control jumped forward, coming to a climax in the 1965 Medicare and Medicaid laws. Curiously, the employer-based format itself reached a peak in the Lyndon Johnson legislation. Since 1965, one president after another has struggled to convert the rest of health insurance to government-based, but always retaining its same general employer-based form. Along the way, two people significantly modified the model: Abraham Flexner, promoting the research-oriented teaching hospital into custodian of the standard of care, replacing the physician guilds; and Henry J. Kaiser, retaining control of a wage cost by calling it a gift, with high corporate income taxes and exempted employee income taxes reducing its effective cost to the employer. In a curious way, high corporate income taxes increased the proportion of healthcare paid for by the Federal Government, by increasing the value of the deduction. Not everyone would agree with this description of history, but I'm convinced of its essence.

Harry Truman

Henry J. Kaiser

Whether the gift comes from business or from government, makes little difference, except to the two contestants. Henry Kaiser seems to have become enlightened that corporate taxation higher than individual rates actually results in important tax advantages for the employer's gift. It allows employers to shift most of the cost to the government, while retaining ultimate control in employers' hands. For many decades the commercial insurance industry tried to break in, but the greatest recent threat to this collusion was accidental. All insurance is a system of cross-subsidies, but the Obama Administration superimposed a subsidy of the poor by the rich, onto an employer system of the young employees subsidizing the older ones. The mismatch between the two seemingly similar subsidies now threatens the coherence of the medical finance system. It also brings out the advantageous warping of the insurance idea by calling it a gift.

Furthermore, the gift is ultimately one of money, so how did service benefits get mixed into this? What does the diagnosis have to do with paying hospital bills, except as a mechanism for obscuring the price? The insurance premiums begin with money, and the insurance intermediary ultimately sends money to the provider of care. Money-in, money-out is what the insurance industry calls **indemnity insurance**. They were using indemnity for centuries before health insurance came along. Why change to a unique and expensive accounting system, if final prices remain unchanged? This device probably started as a way for an insurance intermediary to check the medical validity of a remote claim, but has gradually evolved into an elaborate cost-shifting device. The unfortunate result is to blind the doctors in charge to the true costs of their options. So doctors nowadays totally disregard the posted prices which emerge, when they devise their treatment strategies. The result is very bad, no matter what the original purpose was.

HSA

There may be something to the idea that adding diagnoses and services adds enough mystery to the process to keep away competition, but there are business incentives which seem more central. Now that health cost consumes almost 17% of the gross domestic product, corporate taxes are an important part of

Abraham Flexner

the federal budget, largely explaining why the President might not want to lower them, even driving international businesses to consider moving abroad, rather than lower corporate tax rates. However, if the tax reduction which results from the gift is considered, the net corporate taxes actually paid are not too different from prevailing international rates. If corporate income taxes were eliminated, at least the employer would have to pay for his own wage costs masquerading as gifts. They might even discontinue them, since employers could get the same tax abatement by calling them what they are, wage costs. Following this scenario, the main benefit appears as the tax exemption in the workers' pay package, and the main victims are the competitors who do not receive the gift. If the government is willing to lose the revenue from the tax-paying half of the workforce, they could permit the Health and Retirement Savings Accounts to pay the premiums, essentially providing tax exemption to everyone. If unwilling to lose revenue, the government could start taxing the large employers, which they are now prevented from doing by the seemingly high rates. It's hard to know whom to blame, except this sort of Byzantine structure creates winners and losers, and is ultimately unhealthy.

Two simple and comparatively painless steps -- equalization of tax preferences, and lowering of corporate income taxes -- might soften the objection to indemnity, so why continue the service benefits concept? For this answer you must return to Abraham Flexner, who brought Bismarck's "der herr Professor" system to America, stimulated much research, and ultimately made teaching hospitals vastly more expensive than community hospitals for routine medical care. And now it is necessary to understand the system of calling all activities which are unrelated to patient care "indirect overhead". Although research is largely funded by outside agencies like the NIH and drug companies, it is described as indirect overhead, and distributed among the patient care bills as additional indirect overhead. Unfortunately, a great deal of bloated administrative cost is classified as indirect overhead, as well. No modern corporation could exist without a certain amount of cross-subsidy, but the present amount of it in hospitals is unreasonable. Beyond a certain level, indirect overhead should be forced out of the hospital cross-subsidy system, funded independently, or at least forced into public view. In short, too much routine care is being reimbursed at a high tertiary care level in the teaching hospitals, and this may well stimulate excessive administrative costs as well, even though it may be hard to trace how it comes about. Their competitors in the community hospitals also probably get a little raise, indirectly, to help suppress their complaints. Wall Street was once lambasted for steak dinners and Superbowl tickets from vendors, but you don't hear much about the hospital administrator version.

To make a long story short, service benefits tend to equalize the cost differences between teaching hospitals and community hospitals, ultimately raising the cost of both, but particularly the cost of routine care in teaching hospitals. Historically, this surplus subsidized the research revolution, to which we owe a thirty-year lengthening of our life expectancy. So, go figure. But nevertheless it now blinds physicians as much as the public to the true cost of their medical decisions until they are unable to respond effectively to rising prices, and don't try. A century of it is long enough to devise a better approach, so apparently some pain is needed. But any way you go about lowering them, if you want to control costs, you must start and end with undiluted true costs, not accounting fictions.

How to Live a Long Life and Get Rich

A long time ago, a rich oriental man flew five thousand miles to ask me a question, "What is the secret of long life?" I was so startled by the experience I never did ask him why in the world he would think I knew the answer to such a question. But after a few seconds, I blurted out an answer. "The secret of long life," sez I, " is never get sick." I don't know what his opinion of my profundity was. But I do know what he died of. He was executed by his government, so I hadn't given him the right answer to his question.

At other times, people especially my children, asked me how to get rich. After some practice, I developed a pat answer to that one, too. "The secret of getting rich is to spend less than you earn." What I realized too late to be useful, was that, "Don't get sick and don't spend more than you earn", is a peculiarly American viewpoint, a Philadelphia attitude, and ultimately a Quaker one. It probably explains why there have been so few Pennsylvania Presidents of the United States, few Nobel prize winners, and relatively few Philadelphia glitterati in general.

Because, "Avoid risky behavior" comes closer to the right answer, since risky behavior is a fairly good pathway to glitterati success, and the Quakers had figured out it was a fairly good trade-off, to prefer longevity with prosperity. When I worked at the National Institutes of Health, I was struck by how many eminent scientists went through red lights, and otherwise exhibited risky driving behavior. Everybody knows eminent politicians play around with risky sexual behavior, as do movie stars and glitterati in general. But it is less noticed that America has an even larger proportion of risk avoiders who use that method to live long and prosperously. America has developed an environment where it is possible to get old and prosperous without so much tiresome risk-taking. Kingley's famous text of, "Be good, sweet child, and let who will be clever", doesn't quite get to the root of it. It's risk you want to minimize, not cleverness.

And the verb is minimize, not eliminate. The Quaker term is "steely meekness". And a bothersome American response comes from Winston Churchill, "If the enemy comes, be sure to take one with you."

TOPIC 384 Right Angle Club 2017 => BLOG 3741 Rescuing Medicare from Its Short-Term Thinking.

Rescuing Medicare from Its Short-Term Thinking

Ben Franklin expected a hospital to pay for itself by returning sick people to employment. That misconception runs through medical payments even today.

Instead, our good intentions have created a more expensive problem, with its solutions always just out of reach. **If you live longer, you get more retirement to pay for**, because society also asks for an age limit to employment. Like Franklin we might miss our target, but at least we see the goal. Right now the inevitable consequence of eliminating disease is extension of longevity. Because retirement is continuous while illness comes in episodes, the extra retirement cost (Social Security payments, if you please) might even become more costly than Medicare. Science may eventually cure enough disease to shave costs down to the first and last years of life, starting if possible with the most expensive diseases first. All fine enough, but not right now.

We must **devise a better system than that, which like Health Savings Accounts, could expand from cradle to grave (and 21 years beyond death), generating a surplus by age 65, retaining unused medical surpluses for retirement, and taxable only at death**. Because of compound interest, such a result is actually achievable, but requires a discouraging length of time. We can buy more time with more money, but the public must agree it is worth it.

A lifetime perspective has **six new features**, because we begin with a deficit and end with a surplus: **1)** Passive investing of reserves as a new revenue source **2)** Twenty years of post-mortem Trust Funds to pay for transition **3)** Redeployment of current Medicare payments to individual Health Savings Accounts without changes to its delivery system **4)** Hooking the pieces together on individual Health Savings Accounts like beads on a string, to increase compounding. **5)** Funding retirement with unused augmented Medicare funds, as diseases become cured by science. **6)** Reaching zero balance at age 18, by grandparents half-funding the first 18 years for each of 2.1 grandchildren out of HSA surplus. These are unfamiliar concepts, consuming the rest of this essay.

Unfortunately, even if Congress devises a system to do all this, a century is a long time to leave your money in the hands of strangers. There would be one invariable consequence. Whether money is diverted to bankers' salaries or to aircraft carriers, **rulers always prefer inflation to long term taxes, and sometimes prefer "imperfect agency" to other short term solutions.** Even the Roman Empire eventually succumbed to this conflict. No one oversees other peoples' money as carefully as he would spend his own, so we stand warned by Milton Friedman that your own money management is the only peaceful oversight with a chance of wide-spread success. Even that success depends on running dual systems during transition, one fading out and the other fading in. In the technical section which follows, ways are suggested to manage this dilemma, but above all it seems best to prevent false starts by planning for them. Allow duplication, the ability to make mistakes, and a certain amount of waste from repairing bad choices, as the cost of doing business. Most flaws start as proposed solutions, so it will prove best if winners and losers are widely visible.

This Lifetime Health Savings Account is not a competition of ideologies; it is a series of seemingly unrelated mid-course corrections relating to changing age environments. It leans heavily on putting idle money to work at compound interest, preferably by John Bogle's total market indexing. Even Bogle's system works best with some initial lucky timing. But after a few decades it would scarcely matter when you started, it only matters how much time you have left. Since the beneficiary is dead by the time of settlement, the ones who will really care are those who must pay off the debts. It is up to beneficiaries to fund it, and to educate their descendents to begin early. A single system for everyone will probably never prove universally sensible for hundreds of millions of people. **A voluntary system with age quotas** seems the most painless way to smooth out an admittedly protracted transition. This is a long term plan with short term concessions.

Non-profit systems are not very good at weeding out failures, so for-profit competition is advisable, to speed things up. But anti-trust violation is a common for-profit short-cut, so modern approaches concentrate on preserving competition, not necessarily efficiency. Always remember we probably have plenty of money, never plenty of time. Young people almost never see it that way.

No other large nation has the money or the brashness to attempt so much change all at once, so there are few foreign models. We are pioneers, and costs will be higher for it. Scientists are not fools, they concentrate research on the eight or ten fatal diseases which (they are told) cause 70% of present costs. But several hundred other diseases wait in line, undermining cost prediction for the coming century. Nevertheless, there are only three stages in life with transitions to consider: childhood, working years, and retirement. Two out of these three are dependent on the remaining one at any particular time; but everybody gets a turn. The easiest way to pay for children is for grandparents to donate at death; the best way to pay for retirement is to add compound interest to what we already have saved, and all the rest depends on working people doing more saving, or less spending than they formerly did. There are lots of gimmicks, but that's the basic plan, while we pray for scientists to eliminate the most expensive disease instead of marking time, counting the number of grains of sand on every beach.

A good plan uses demonstration projects and accepts the possibility of occasionally slowing down. Research and development can be costly at first, before costs eventually decline. We may be--or may not be-- as lucky as we were with heart attacks, in which the commonest cause of death was greatly diminished by a daily aspirin tablet. Or we may struggle on as we did with pernicious anemia and diabetes. Both diseases are treated with injections discovered almost a century ago. But pernicious anemia is treated at trivial cost while diabetes struggles as the most expensive chronic disease we have, prolonging life but not extinguishing cost. Only Americans would plunge ahead anyway, while a President would be foolish to try to change deep cultural attitudes too rapidly. We are warned not to see ourselves as exceptional, but we do see ourselves as exceptional, no matter what the facts.

The facts are the Medicare age group has most of the costs, younger people generate most of the savings. Third rail or not, the problem is to manage **a gigantic funds transfer between generations**, while avoiding imperfect agents who divert money to their own purposes. In some ways it is more a financial problem than a medical one. We watch private insurance pay its executives multimillion dollar salaries, and we watch our government divert medical money for battleships and babysitting. It is time to stop watching, and try **modified individual ownership**, putting our idle money back to work. **Saving our own money for our own retirement if given a choice, instead of forcibly moving money among demographic groups of strangers**. Choices should be voluntary and for-profit, so people will actually notice which approach works best, and then switch to it when convinced. This being political, some people will put their thumbs on the scale. But this being America, the public will not be fooled for long.

So this summarizes the idea. What follows is a general outline of vital technical details for pulling it off.

TOPIC 384 Right Angle Club 2017 => BLOG 3818 Tax Legislation--Just A Condominium Squabble

Tax Legislation--Just A Condominium Squabble
New blog 2017-11-11 02:52:56 description

Congress meets every year and, almost every year, most Americans are more interested in athletic games. People who make politics their profession may be more involved more of the time, but eventually it is taxes which supply the force to involve the public. Occasionally it is the Constitution, but the Constitution mainly establishes structure, and people are generally satisfied with the present structure. There is limited time for debate, and to tell the truth, limited patience for it so the party leadership is left with the power to manipulate timing around holidays And the leaders organise the limited "floor" time carefully to preserve their control of it. Right now is one of those corners of our time, when an important issue gets crowded next to a holiday recess, the issue gets explained to the public, and public opinion is closely divided at first. It all sounds familiar, but there are important particularities.

Constitution

Everybody is affected, everybody thinks he knows what George Washington thought. We had once just finished the Revolutionary War, almost losing that war because we had so much trouble agreeing to tax ourselves, to defend and govern ourselves thereby. When the Continental Congress abandoned Philadelphia to the British in 1779, only Robert Morris stayed behind as acting President, and never forgot the dreadful experience of governing without a government. In fact, about five future Constitutional delegates were trapped by an angry mob in the upper floors of James Wilson's house at the so-called Battle of "Fort Wilson". There was no need for these patriots to debate later about the need for taxes, law or order. This experience settled the tax issue for them, permanently.

Revolutionary War

A whole host of tax issues are vitally important to someone somewhere, but the tax issue dominates almost all three hundred million citizens of every age and occupation. lowering by how much is desirable for corporate taxes, and lowering by how much is ideal for federal taxes shared with state and local governments. Corporations were then a new and unanticipated way to run a business, and generally a more efficient way, although not a perfect one. About half the country half-believes it is urgent to go in opposite directions on details, and divide in opposite directions on a subject, but the other half is suspicious of some hidden agenda. There probably isn't enough slack in the systems to do split the difference. If we try to change, we dispute how much to change. In this case, we have the example of southern Ireland, which went too far in lowering corporate taxes to 12.5% in a single step. It seems simple enough, but we dispute who gets the credit, and most of the leadership is fearful of getting too far ahead of the public. The Civil War is the only time in our history when compromise wasn't sufficient, and in retrospect it probably might have been handled without a war.

The result needs improvement because of repeated patching, so simplification is desirable but not paramount. It would be nice to stop gerrymandering, but no one proposes a feasible way, as is true of the narrow balance between the two parties. It is clear that the Congressional power of the purse is weakened by overspending the budget and then demanding that we avoid a default by funding an unauthorized deficit. Since it is unclear how to accomplish these three structural approaches peacefully, we probably can't do them. So we will probably resort to half-measures, with fuller measures after we can see what happens. The risk is that the North Koreans, or the Saudi princes, or the defeated Russians, or some other foreign power will solve the problem for us in the meantime. This approach amounts to buying some time by surrendering some control, and we may be sorry we did it. But we keep on building more condominiums, so it must have some utility.

The Civil War

TOPIC 384 Right Angle Club 2017 => BLOG 3502 Revolutionary Features of Big Data

Revolutionary Features of Big Data
New blog 2016-03-20 17:34:08 description

The Right Angle Club, now luxuriating in its new quarters in the Pyramid Club, was recently visited by Professor Kenneth Burdett of University of Pennsylvania and Cornell. A charming fellow with a Scottish burr in his accent (he mentioned he had been born in England), he elected to tell us of a new revolution in economics which has slipped by us unnoticed, without textbooks devoted to it, or Nobel Prizes awarded. That is, many of the concepts central to macroeconomics are really net values, or ratios between two more basic facts. The concept of unemployment was offered as a handy example.

Professor Kenneth Burdett

We tend to think of 230,000 new jobs this month as a hard fact, but it is actually a ratio of several million people getting new jobs, and several million losing jobs, not to mention a number who simply decide to leave the workforce and retire. We all sort of knew it was a ratio, but most of us had no idea it was the net flow of many-times larger numbers. It is because of the difference in the size of the flows, which are much greater in size than the small net unemployment figure, that this is a revolution rather than a humdrum ratio. We've been accustomed to the much smaller ratio than to the many-times larger flow numbers. What

Mark Rank

happens is vastly larger numbers of people lose their jobs during a depression, but millions more people re-enter the workforce, too, probably at a lower wage level.

Curiously, a new book by Mark Rank of Washington University, and Thomas A. Hirschl of Cornell (!), called *Chasing the American Dream: Understanding What Shapes our Fortunes* has just appeared, saying the same thing. Their approach is to develop a figure for the risk of being unemployed for a year in the next 5, 10, or 15, and at the moment the answer for unmarried white persons sometime during the next fifteen years in the future is 32 percent. That seems to be a much more scary projection than to set the present aggregate total unemployment at 4.6%. We'll have to wait 15 years to see if that prediction really is accurate, or if it has the dire consequences we immediately assign to it. But it would appear many assumptions are about to be set on their head, and the quality of our projections is about to shift dramatically. For example, Chairman Bernanke of the Federal Reserve placed great stock on wage inflation being "core" inflation, but these calculations suggest much more can be made of the data than that. Since somehow it is calculated the present recession has eight more years to run, because current oversupply will require eight more years to run down, data recalculated in this new way may give different answers. It would then be useful to see which is the better approach to economic prediction.

Thomas A. Hirschl

Chasing the American Dream

Right Angle members who lean both right and left seemed impressed and befuddled by this new view of an old topic, and that's probably a very good thing. There seems no question of the validity of the approach, no question of significance, and little doubt of its ability to change attitudes. We look forward to many more insights from the Dismal Science, of this nature. For instance, this professor of many students of the *rentier* class remarked at how repeatedly he had been struck by students able to afford red convertibles (and the Princeton tuition cost) were nevertheless willing to throw themselves into the scrum of Wall Street, to make even more money. He regarded that as a strength of the American economy, in stark contrast to that in Europe, where the first sign of prosperity sent his old acquaintances, straight to the pub to relax a bit. In the British aristocracy, "entering trade" is a low-class thing to do, whereas sitting on the sidewalk sipping wine is the mark of really high class.

www.ingramcontent.com/pod-product-compliance
Lightning Source LLC
Chambersburg PA
CBHW081355040426
42451CB00017B/3462